THE KELLY GANG,

OR,

The Outlaws of the Wombat Ranges

Be cautious what you say, of whom, and to whom

———————

GEORGE WILSON HALL

ETT IMPRINT, SYDNEY

This edition published by ETT Imprint, Exile Bay 2022

First published by G. Wilson Hall,
Proprietor of the
Mansfield Guardian 1879

Published by ETT Imprint in 2015, reprinted 2017, 2019.

ETT IMPRINT
PO Box R1906
Royal Exchange NSW 1225
Australia

Copyright © this edition ETT Imprint 2015, 2022

ISBN 978-1-922698-54-4 (paper)
ISBN 978-1-922698-55-1 (ebook)

Cover: An original carte-de-visite showing Dan Kelly, Ned Kelly and Steve Hart on a verandah at Echuca, 1879. Kelly Family Collection.

Design by Hanna Gotlieb

*Portrait of Ned with Dan (left) and Steve (not Byrne) in 1879
photographed by Carl Burrows, but not released till July 1880.*

PREFACE

We take it for granted that in the present excited state of public feeling among all classes on the subject of the now notorious "Kelly Gang", no apology is needed for offering to the community the accompanying narrative, though hurriedly thrown together and, therefore, inevitably liable to animadversion on the score of its shortcomings.

What has been chiefly aimed at in the little volume is the compilation of as truthful, and at the same time readable, a story as possible under the circumstances, from the best and most reliable sources at our command; and we would take this opportunity of fully admitting our obligations, not only to the journals of the day, but more especially to certain individuals, who, without being named here, will be sure to recognise the acknowledgement, being those from whom interesting and important particulars, unobtainable elsewhere, were gleaned, as well as confirmation of various previously published items of intelligence.

When we assure our readers that we received a great part of our information from the very best authorities, and that, to say the least, no pains have ever been spared in travelling for its collection, with that view, we give, by inference, but a meagre idea of the great difficulties we have had to contend with at the outset of our enterprise.

Doubtless, the book will be found open to the charge of faultiness in style, while that kind of word-painting, which enhances the interest of so many descriptive efforts in other works, and is so dear to numerous readers, as well as several writers, will be found conspicuous by its absence.

In some parts of the history, too, an unavoidable hiatus will be met with, because we prefer submitting to the charge of incompleteness rather than fill such gaps with materials supplied by imagination alone.

Yet, while deprecating failure, we modestly venture to anticipate that the humble barque which we have, with an amount of temerity, launched upon the treacherous billows of public opinion, will not become at once at utter wreck upon the rocks or quicksands of unjust adverse criticism, and, at the same time, we are prepared to bow before the unbiased utterances of matured judgement relative to the many blemishes almost inevitable in a work hastily constructed, and by comparatively un-practiced hands.

With impartiality as our guiding star, we have endeavoured, and we trust successfully, to avoid the Scylla of falsely exaggerating the atrocities of the outlaws, sufficiently terrible in their actuality, and at the same time not be drawn into the vortex of the more dangerous Charybdis of being adjudged, be it never so erroneously, sympathisers with that fearful band.

There requires no aggravation of the bare reality to intensify, for example, the horrors of the dreadful tragedy enacted on the never-to-be-forgotten 26th of October 1878, amid the recesses of the Wombat Ranges; and, again, it would be equally unjust to our readers, and derogatory to our own integrity, were we, by silence, to appear to acquiesce in various unsubstantial charges which, either based only on suspicion or mayhap, born of invective genius, have been circulated, in good faith no doubt, by various publishers against the malefactors and their unfortunate connections.

"A plain, unvarnished tale" of the facts will be found in places sufficiently shocking to satisfy, if not cloy, the most morbidly voracious appetite for the horrible sensational. We have, therefore, in the production of the following relation, as equitable historians, adopted for our motto –
"Nothing extenuate, nor set down aught in malice".
- THE AUTHORS

MELBOURNE, 22nd February, 1879.

CHAPTER I

"Now lithe and listen, gentles all,
The while I do unfold
The parentage and eke the deeds
Of Rob, the outlaw bold;
And how he drove the keepers
By mountain, moor and glen;
And how he held the forest, free,
With all his lusty men.".

- Old Ballad

If imitation be truly described as the sincerest flattery, surely we may also assume it to be a mark of the most genuine admiration; hence, being totally incapable of producing anything remotely approaching his style, we cannot be said to go far astray in adopting the plan followed by one of England's most celebrated classical authors, Henry Fielding, when composing the life of "JONATHAN WILD, THE GREAT", which plan is thus referred to in one of the introductory chapters to the work;–

It is the custom of all biographers, at their entrance into their work, to step a little backwards (as far indeed as they are able), and to trace up their hero, as the ancients did the river Nile, till an incapacity of proceeding higher puts an end to their search.

What first gave rise to this method is somewhat difficult to determine. But whatever origin this custom had, it is now too well established to be disputed. I shall therefore conform to it in the strictest manner.

At the latter end of the year of our Lord one thousand eight hundred and thirty-nine, a family of the name of Quin, numbering eight persons, and hailing from the neighbourhood of Belfast, Ireland, landed on the shores of Hobson's Bay, from the good ship England, having come out as Government emigrants, with a view to bettering their condition at Port Phillip, which at that time was looked on by the inhabitants of the "Old Country" almost as terra incognita.

The family consisted of James and Mary Quin, the parents, with six children – namely, Patrick, who was afterwards accidentally drowned at Echuca, in 1850; Mary Anne, since deceased; John; Ellen, destined to give birth to the outlawed Kellys; Katherine and Jane.

The Quins, on their arrival, settled in what is the Melbourne of the present day, and remained there for some short time, the father supporting his family by working as a porter at different commercial establishments, until, by frugality and industry, he succeeded in accumulating sufficient funds to enable him to rent some land, and make a purchase of a few milch cows and bullocks. His first venture was on a small farm at Brunswick, where, in a limited hut comfortable homestead, Mrs Quin carried on the business of dairying to a profitable extent, while her husband added to the domestic store from the profits of carting with his bullocks on the roads, and cultivating a moderate portion of his holding.

After a short time, having prospered reasonably well in his undertakings, he shifted to Broadmeadows, where he rented 1,280 acres of land, which he devoted to grazing and cultivation purposes; and the sons, Patrick and John, being by this time old enough to take charge of his teams, he was enabled to turn his undivided attention to the engagement of the farm.

Before this, the number of his children had been increased by nine, by the successive births of William, Margaret and Grace.

After a few years of renumerated industry in this locality, he removed his quarters to a section of land (640 acres), at the head of the Merri Creek, near Wallan-Wallan, which he rented from a man name James Cameron, and upon which, with increased stock, he continued his previous occupations, carrying on the dairy operations in a far more extensive way; prosperity, as before, attending his efforts. The neighbourhood at the time was known as Kemp's Swamp.

Shortly after breaking out of the diggings, in 1851, he was enobled, in consequence of the increased value of stock, and other reasons, to purchase 700 acres adjoining his holding, and partly situated where the Wallan-Wallan railway station now stands, and here he continued to pursue his usual vocations, with the addition of dealing in and breeding horses and cattle.

He remained on this property until the year 1865, and, with the remaining portion of his family, was universally respected – he and they were in their former locations – for honesty, industry and kindness, Mrs Quin being especially an object of sincere regard, on account of the unwearying and profuse hospitality she used to display, not only to her friends and aquaintances, but also to every tired, indignant, or benighted wayfaring stranger who might call at her door. Indeed, she carried this comparatively rare and admirable propensity, almost to the verge of what might be termed a weakness, and was continued, we are informed, to act the good Samaritan whenever occasion demanded, as far as in her power lay, up to the date of the present memoir, so that we may reasonably conclude the amiable peculiarity will not cease to influence her during the remainder of her earthly career.

In 1865, however, desiring to become owner of a squatting station, Quin, having sold his Wallan-Wallan property to considerable advantage, purchased a run at the head of the King River, to which he transferred his large stock of cattle, horses, brood mares, &c. – a spot that afterwards became famous as the place near which Power, the bushranger, was captured while asleep in his gunyah.

Not many years after the purchase – about 1869 – James Quin died; and shortly afterwards, the sons having disposed of the station, the remaining members became scattered, Mrs. Quin finding a home with a married daughter, with whom she now resides.

We must now request our readers to accompany us retrospectively and imaginatively to Donnybrook, near the Merri Creek, in the year 1849, with a view to the introduction of the father of the outlawed Kellys.

John Kelly, better known as "Red Kelly", in contradistinction to a man who rejoiced in the soubriquet of "Black Kelly", and to whom he was not in any way related, arrived, not very long before the time above indicated, from Tasmania, on the completion of his sentence, to which hell-ipon-earth for convicts he had been transported from Ireland for a term of fifteen years.

He was a native of the Emerald Isle, having been born and reared in that particular county which the poet described in the following laudatory strain:–

"The sweetest sod that e'er was trod
By Sassenach or fairy;
Show me the land that can compare
With darlint Tipperary."

And it may not, therefore, prove so much a matter of surprise to learn that his enforced expatriation originated in a charge of being concerned either in a faction fight or some other affray at a fair, during which one of the combatants, as was not at all unusual in those days, came to an untimely end.

The illegal act, however, on account of which he was banished beyond the seas, would not in any country, even now, be ranked in the category of disgraceful crimes, much less in a part of the world where it would have been viewed by the country people in a more harmless light than the permanent removal of a tyrannical and obnoxious landlord, a bailiff, a process-server, a gauger, or an informer – the last of whom would occupy, in public estimation, a place immeasurably lower than the Melbourne professional hangman and flagellator, the notorious Gately, does among the Victorian population. In this colony, moreover, he was subsequently convicted of being in unlawful possession of certain beef, for which he failed to satisfactorily account, and for this received a sentence of six months' imprisonment, which he suffered.

It is our duty, as faithful chroniclers, to state the noticeable fact that this John Kelly was always, in this colony at any rate, remarked as a rather timid man, averse to quarrelling, and ever prone to act the part of a peacemaker when he saw others engaged in any altercation calculated to lead to violence.

These, notwithstanding the many accusations with which his memory has been so freely bespattered, are the only two charges that have been brought home to him. It is, therefore, fully in accordance with the British principles of justice to give him the benefit of any doubt that can exist as to whatever delinquencies have been asserted or inferred to his prejudice.

At any rate, about the period we are writing of, John or "Red" Kelly was engaged in splitting and fencing, near the Merri Creek, and chancing to be in a hotel at Donnybrook, in the vicinity of James Quin's residence, enjoying the customary relaxation after a hard week's work, he for the first time encountered the latter individual, with whom he dropped into conversation over a friendly nobbler.

During the progress of their discourse, the subject of the manufacture of illicit whisky was brought on the board and duly discussed, Kelly informing his colloquist that he was fully and practically acquainted with the art and mystery of distillation. At last, after eloquently expatiating on the certain profits derivable from that industry, and argumentatively pointing out the immunity from discovery offered by the features of the neighbouring ranges, he proposed that Quin should go into partnership with him in the purchase and working of a "jigger still".

To this proposition Quin, as on several future occasions, steadily refused to lend an ear; but the meeting of the evening was the commencement of an intimacy which finally gained Kelly admission, on the grounds of acquaintanceship, to the farmer's home. Shortly afterwards, some of the neighbouring residents, whose avarice was tickled by the golden prospects held out, and really believed in, by Kelly, joined him in the bush-whis-key speculation, with the speedy and almost inevitable result of complete failure of the venture.

Within a brief space following the meeting at the hotel, Kelly commenced to pay his addresses to Ellen Quin, but altogether in opposition to the wishes of her parents, who, not considering him a desirable match, refused him point blank when he asked their permission to marry their daughter. But this denial did not practically carry that weight with it which, theoretically, such rejections are supposed to do; for the suitor, with the address and impetuosity of a true Irishman in love-making, soon brought the object of his affections to consent to a runaway match, and, on the day following their elopement to Melbourne, they were there irrevocably joined in the bonds of holy wedlock.

On their return to the Merri Creek, the old folks, sensibly recognizing the futility of making any fuss about so every-day an occurrence, forgave the delinquents, but instead of inviting them to take up the residence under the parental roof, they permitted their newly-acquired son-in-law, who was an expert bush-carpenter, to erect a dwelling for himself and wife on a portion of their land.

Here, in the snug little hut, the young couple resided until the breaking out of the diggings, the husband pursuing his adopted calling of splitter and fencer.

Ellen Kelly (nee Quin)

CHAPTER II

"What is here?
Gold-yellow, glittering, precious gold."
- Shakespeare

At length, yielding, as thousands of others did at that time and afterwards, to the temptations held out by the golden visions which the highly-coloured reports from the Australian El Dorado conjured up before his imagination, Kelly proceeded to try his luck on the fields where fortune was said to smile upon all, showering riches particularly on those who sued for her favours pick in hand.

Bendigo was the stage upon which he made his debut in the character of a gold-digger, and there, in a short space of time, his anticipations were realised to a sufficiently satisfactory extent to justify his return home.

After coming back, he for some time dealt in horses, which soon increased his original "pile" enough to allow of his purchasing a comfortable farm at Beveridge. He remained here for a number of years, but eventually sold out and removed to a farm which he rented between Avenel and Tabilk. He chose this locality in preference to taking up his residence in more unsettled parts, where he could have secured better land on more advantageous terms, because it supplied the necessity of propinquity to a public school, and Kelly was most solicitous that his children should enjoy the benefit of some place of instruction.

At this place the head of the family died, leaving issue three sons, namely – Edward and Daniel (the outlaws); and James, who is undergoing a sentence of stealing some horses, which he afterwards sold to Mr. Dixon, of Wangaratta; and three daughters – one married to Alexander Gunn, and since deceased; one married to William Skillion, now in jail on a conviction of being concerned in an assault on a constable; and one, Kate, the youngest, still single.

Some eleven or twelve years ago, the Kellys gave up the Avenel farm, and removed to a piece of land on the Eleven-Mile Creek, about four miles from Greta township, where they built a small house, which was kept as a shanty or house of accommodation. At the time of leaving Avenel the sons were aged as follows:– Edward about 12, James 9, and Daniel 6 or 7; and since that time, as soon as they were old enough, the ostensible occupations of the two elder sons have been horse-breaking and farm and station work, while the youngest one generally assisted his mother and sister at home – all of them occasionally indulging in horse-dealing and swapping.

It is a significant fact, that although according to various public journals and the statements of several private individuals this place, its occupants, and its visitors were of exceptionally evil repute, yet there is absolutely no record whatever of any stolen property having been traced to its precincts, nor have any instances of what is known as "lambing down", such as have founded and helped to build the fortunes of some men now in good and reputable positions, been brought to light in connection with the establishment.

There is little doubt that Morgan, Power, and other desperadoes may have made it a house of call in their excursions, as they did many other out-of-the-way shanties; but so, also, did many harmless travellers in journeying through that district, as well as sundry of that numerous class whole claim to respectability is chiefly based upon the fact of their never having been found out in the perpetration of any nefarious fact. But this affords not the slightest excuse for the sheltering of marauders, cattle-reevers, and highwaymen by the owners of the shanty, nor can it be reasonably imagined that they could have harboured these abominable plunderers and malefactors – if they did so – without, to a certain extent, sympathizing and approving of their lawless acts; unless, indeed, the proprietors were under the tyranny of a similar terrorism to that which has since been attributed to the Kellys in their bushranging career, and which, if true, may possibly have been suggested to those notorious outlaws by the example of the older offenders.

As, however, we have no sufficient proof to guide out judgment in the matter, we must be content to record the rumours and facts at our disposal, leaving our readers to form their own conclusions.

Ned Kelly, aged 15.

CHAPTER III

"Small habits, well pursued, betimes
May reach the dignity of crimes."
– Butler

The published assertion that the younger Kellys were brought up as thieves by their father is altogether without foundation in fact, whatever boyish depredations they may have indulged in having been carried out on their "own hook", and without the concurrence of their parents.

Some of the stories that have been circulated since their entry upon a career of murder and robbery, purportion to illustrative of their juvenile escapades, are not only, as far as we can learn by inquiry, totally unsustainable by any kind of evidence, but many of them amusingly incredible in their details.

One selection will amply serve as an average example of the ridiculous and contemptible rubbish they are composed of. It is, in outline, as follows, and the minor details may be made to vary according to the fancy or inventive capacity of each retailer of the anecdote:–

In the outskirts of a village not a hundred miles from Avenel, through which the younger Kellys, when boys, were in the habit of passing, there dwelt – in a humble cottage – neatly furnished, and situated in a nice little orchard – an elderly widowed female with an only son, who, though she had a comfortable little income secured to her, sufficient for the ordinary wants of a person in her station, yet felt like the old woman in the alms-house, who, while admitting to the visiting clergyman the many mercies, including tea and snuff, she had to thank Heaven for, qualified her expression of gratitude by declaring that the Lord took it out of herin corns.

Now, the dame in our story suffered a counterpoise to her blessings in the shape of a chronic rheumatism, and – jointly with her young hopeful, who was an embryo shoemaker with a club foot – a constant dread that the larrikins and larrikinesses of the neighbourhood would make a ride upon her garden, to the loss of the

Nectarine fruits which the compliant boughs
Yielded them, sidelong, as they sat

and by the sale of which she was wont to supplement her modest revenue, and thus was enabled, not only to put by a penny for a rainy day, but also to indulge in sundry extras of feminine adornment as well as table comforts, otherwise beyond her reach. For age could not altogether wither her vanity, nor custom stale the infinite variety her palate craved continually.

She might have made a much better market of her produce than she did, had she but established, as she was often advised, a little fruit stall in the village, on the borders of which she hung; but, alas! her rheumatism and, above all, her conceit, forbade her presiding over so unassuming a Temple of Pomons, and her son, though even more grasping than his ma, also permitted his vanity to overcome his avarice in a similar manner, and indignantly refused all entreaties to become what he flippantly designated "book-keeper to an apple-stand". As to engaging a regular "fruiterer's assistant" on a small scale, it was altogether out of the question, because they believed, not only that the legitimate expenses would more than swallow up the probable profits, but also that their deputy would be sure to rob them when he got a chance. The latter theory they held, for various reasons best known to themselves, in connection with any and everyone who might have an opportunity of being profitably dishonest without detection. This well-assorted pair, moreover, affected the sentimental, and professed, as well as persuaded themselves, that they were ardent admirers of Byron's, Moore's, Longfellows, and Tennyson's poems, extracts from which, by turns, the son used dutifully to read to his parents during the evenings, for, sooth to say, her eyesight was not as good as in the palmy days of her youth. She, therefore, for this and many other reasons, had cause to congratulate herself that the lad had enjoyed considerable educational advantages, which he was not loth to display. There was one poem on particular of Tennyson's that seemed to possess a strange and horrible attraction for them, namely, "Walking to the Mail", but which, nevertheless, they seem to shudder at when that part was reached commencing – "There lived a dayflint near; we stole his fruit". This, though, has nothing to do with the point of the story.

One day a young lad, or boy, of the neighbourhood, who was slowly recovering from a long and severe attack of Ophthalmia, and was still half blind, happened to wheel an infant sister of his to the dame's garden, in a little perambulator, improvised from a gin case, on four wooden wheels, in order to keep a promise of "shouting" threepennyworth of plums for that interesting innocent. Suddenly, after weighing out the fruit and pocketing the coppers, an inspiration seemed to strike the proprietor of the Eden, and she said, "What are you doing now, Jim?" "Nothink, please marm", replied the youth; "the doctor says as 'ow I haint to do nothin' till my Heyes is well". "Well, Jim", rejoined the artful she, "I can give you an easy job that won't hurt your eyes, if you like; you might as well be wheeling fruit as flesh and blood, you know, and if you like to hawk some of this fruit round for sale, I'll give you - let me see – I'll give you, well, a penny out of every shilling of your takings – no credit mind, all cash." Now, if Jim had been a vulgar boy, or addressing one of the common inhabitants of the place, he would probably have said, "It's a whack, ole gal; I'm on". But such not being the case, he politely observed, "Thankee, marm, I'll be hup to-morrer mornin' hearly; 'taint much, I know, but its better nor nothin'". And as he turned to go, the widow, by way of clinching the bargain, cut a small slice off a little apple she had commenced peeling, and handing it to him, said, "All right, don't forget, like a good boy. So long."

Like a good boy, sure enough, the industrious Jim put in an early appearance the following morning, and, when the fruit had been weighed out, to the half ounce, he received his instructions as to the most likely places to call at, and the different prices to ask at each. Then, as Jim was starting to make his first essay as a commission agent, the son of the house came along and said, "Look here, Jim, we'll deduct the value of any fruit you lose, or can't account for, from your profits, at selling price, that's all". Jim started in excellent spirits; but – alas for the vanity of all human aspirations – at the bottom of a hill, on an unfrequented part of the road to the village, two of the Kellys met him, and seeing that he was helpless and smaller than themselves, they agreed to attack and spoil him at once. Jim showed what fight he could, but soon had to yield to superior numbers, weight, age, and eyesight. The highwayboys then, after rolling him in the dust and kicking him severely, took as much fruit as they could eat and carry, and upsetting the "convaniency", kicked the reminder about the road, leaving the weeping costermonger to collect the debris, if worth it, and calculate how long it would take him to make good the loss at his moderate percentage of remuneration. What made the act more atrocious was that the Kellys were on intimate terms with the widow and her son.

This is the story as detailed to us, but without any attempt to make us believe it; on the other hand, it was laid before us for the same reason as we venture to present it to the reader – namely, as a sample of what inconceivable "rot" can be invented, and what absurdly improbable and inhuman acts can be attributed even to boys, under certain circumstances, just as celebrated wits have jests and bon mots fathered on them, which they not only did not originate, but, in all probability, never even heard.

CHAPTER IV

"I strike quickly, being moved".
– Romeo and Juliet

The majority of the many convictions recorded against the Kellys, as well as their blood-relations, the Quins, appear to have been of the "assault and battery" description, and form a long and varied list, which may not appear extraordinary to those who know them and are acquainted with the highly excitable and ungovernable temperament which seems to be one of the chief characteristics of the family.

Naturally impatient of restraint, and of uncontrollable passions when aroused, they have, in many cases, given way to acts to lawless violence under circumstances of aggravation – and, in some instances, exceptional provocation – which to persons of more lymphatic constitutions might seem unpardonable, and for which the law admits of no excuse, and rarely palliation.

The list of their proven offences is not, however, limited to such misdemeanours, which seem to have been distributed pretty freely and impartially among the Quins and the Kellys, and are of such a number and similarity as would render a recapitulation of them tedious, monotonous and uninteresting.

It will be sufficient to relate that one of the cases of violent assault happened in this wise. A brother seeing another brother set upon by a number of assailants, seized upon a bullock-yoke to do battle in his defence. With this simple but impressive weapon he emulated the performance of Samson when operating on the Philistines with the jaw-bone of an ass; and he succeeded, not only in rescuing his brother, but also in gaining a three months' retirement amid the peaceful shades of Beechworth jail, by the end of which visit he might be expected to have recovered the energy which he had lavishly expended in his brother's defence. A stirrup-iron, on another occasion, proved as effective and trustworthy weapon in the face of odds.

These instances refer more particularly to the Quin branch, and are therefore only incidentally introduced in a narrative which ought to be confined to the Kellys proper, who, in truth, used to indulge in the excitement of a free fight or a select punching match as often as might be expected from their fiery dispositions.

But it was not until 1871 that the police succeeded in establishing "a case" against Edward Kelly, when he received a sentence of three years' imprisonment in Beechworth assizes, for receiving, with a guilty knowledge, a horse stolen from the postmaster at Mansfield. James Kelly, another brother is, at the date of writing, undergoing his maiden sentence for horse-stealing, while Daniel has never yet been what is technically called "lagged", although he has undergone his fair share of punishment for minor offences. A warrant which was issued for his apprehension in April last, on a charge of horse-stealing, has formed a starting point, from which it would appear other circumstances have led up to the frightful massacre of police at the Wombat, with the daring and unscrupulous, though bloodless robberies, which have followed that deplorable event.

CHAPTER V

"They fell on; I made good my place; at length they came to the broomstaff with me. I defied them still; when suddenly a file of boys came behind them, loose shot, delivered such a shower of pebbles, that I was fain to draw mine honour in and let them win the work".
– King Henry VIII

On the 15th of April, 1878, Constable Fitzpatrick, who was stationed at Benalla, proceeded, according to his own account, to Greta, for the purpose of arresting Daniel Kelly for horse-stealing, on a warrant, which he confessed he had not with him, and had never seen, but the existence of which he took for granted from a notice in the Police Gazette. Whether he took this course by command of his superiors, or on his own responsibility, does not, we believe, appear.

On reaching the abode of the Kellys he made a prisoner of Dan, but, with ill-judged leniency, permitted him to partake of some supper as a preliminary to his journey to Benalla.

During the domiciliary visit, William Williamson and William Skillion being present, a row ensued, in the course of which the constable was knocked down by Mrs. Kelly with a shovel, and shot in the wrist by Edward while on the ground and in the hands of all the others. A consultation was held among the party as to how to dispose of their prisoner, and murder was freely discussed; but in the end mercy prevailed, and after forcing Fitzpatrick to extract the bullet from his wrist with a pocket knife, and making him promise solemnly not to divulge what had occurred, they allowed him to depart.

After riding some distance, he heard two men galloping after him helter-skelter, which he interpreted to mean a change of views on the part of some of his late assailants, and an intention to secure his silence by death.

Being well mounted he succeeded in escaping, under cover of the darkness, and having arrived in safety at head-quarters, and not considering himself bound by the promise he had made to save his life, at once reported the particulars of the event.

Upon an information to that effect, Mrs. Kelly, W. Williamson and W. Skillion were subsequently arrested, but Dan made good his escape, after promising his mother that he would never suffer himself to be taken alive; and was soon after joined by his brother Edward.

Mrs. Kelly, W. Williamson, and Skillion were committed for trial to Beechworth, where they were convicted of a murderous assault on the police, and were sentenced by Sir Redmond Barry to imprisonment for terms of three, six and six years respectively, on the evidence of Constable Fitzpatrick. Furthermore, a reward of £100 was offered for the apprehension of Ned Kelly, to whom it was intimated that had he stood beside his mother in the dock, he would have received a sentence of 21 years, an item of news that certainly did not tend to increase the probability of his openly visiting the busy haunts of men.

CHAPTER VI

―――――

"Either envy, therefore, or misprision
Is guilty of this fault, and not my son".
― Shakespeare

The story, however, of the occurrence as narrated by the opposite side, presents the scene in a very different aspect – an aspect too, that, to any observer of human nature, especially in these colonies, does not offer to the view any features bearing the stamp of utter impossibility imprinted on their surface.

The Kelly party aver, then, that Fitzpatrick, "pretty well on", as it is termed, came across William Skillion, near Mrs. Kelly's place, and entered into interrogative conversation with him relative to splitting upon Crown lands without a licence, and that, during the chat the constable inquired the whereabouts of Dan from Skillion, who, not scenting any danger, replied that the former was at home. The two then proceeded to the house, where Fitzpatrick arrested the younger Kelly for horse-stealing. Ned not being present at the time, not at any future time that day.

Being a sort of acquaintance of the family, the constable could not well refuse to permit Dan to get some refreshment previous to starting, and his captor followed suit as far as a liquid "revivifier" or two went.

The report continues, that while the meal was in progress, or immediately after its conclusion, Kelly asked to see the warrant for his apprehension, which he was entitled to do, and that Fitzpatrick, not having the document with him, as he afterwards admitted, became insulting and bullying, and attempted to put the "darbies" on Dan.

Maternal affection then, which in some cases would be lauded, and described as one of the holiest and best instincts implanted in the human breast, urged the mother to the defence of her son, who, guilty or not guilty, as it appeared to her was about to be illegally arrested, so, seizing an old shovel from the fireplace, she applied it to the constable's helmet, or cap, with a power that was at least equal to the force of her arm, added to the weight of the shovel, multiplied by the velocity of that improvised weapon as it fell. Fitzpatrick, as may be anticipated, came to the ground confused from the joint affects of the "licker" and the "lick", and while striving to recover the perpendicular, he drew his revolver, in the clumsy handling of which, in the midst of general scrimmage, a chamber was accidentally discharged, the ball from which wounded him slightly in the wrist.

Mrs. Kelly, Dan, and the rest of the company then rejected him and saw no more of him that night.

In some quarters it was asserted that the constable did not go to Kellys' with any intention of arresting Dan, but simply to make a call, and that, being resisted in attempting forcibly to take undue and unwelcome liberties with a member of the family, he sought revenge by attempting to capture the brother, producing his handcuffs to show his authority, and so forth. The rest of the story as before. The latter report, as the newspaper would say, required confirmation, though it agrees with a statement made subsequently by Edward Kelly at Jerilderie.

Be the truth as it may, the affair is admitted by those who ought to know, to be to a great extent involved in mystery, and the general opinion is, in any case, that the constable did not altogether act "the clean potato". If it were the fact – but we are far from saying that it was so – that he was guilty of any wilful misfeasance of falsehood whereby the parties concerned might have been wrongly convicted, we would not envy him his feelings when he reflected (as under these hypothetical circumstances he would be bound to do) on the trebly murderous result of his action, so say nothing of the years of misery and degradation entailed on persons innocent of the charge brought against them, merely to screen himself from merited punishment, or mayhap, only reprimand.

Of course, as law-fearing, law-abiding and law-supporting subjects, we are supposed to believe that, even if the constable did, under exceptional circumstances, slightly overstep the regulated bounds of duty or veracity, yet he is to be almost excused on the universally adopted, though not generally acknowledged, principle that the end justifies the means.

Constable Fitzpatrick

CHAPTER VII

"He was a pal o' mine,
My dear boy –"
– Modern Song

Edward Kelly was at one time charged with being an accomplice and mate of the notorious Harry Power, who for so many years, though ill and long past middle age, bid defiance, single handed, to the police in the North-Eastern District, but for reasons which it would be a breach of confidence to both sides to reveal, sufficient evidence was brought forward to ensure his conviction.

Power, in conversation with "the Vagabond", at Pentridge, stigmatized Edward Kelly as cowardly and bloodthirsty, and said that he was afraid to perform the simple act of holding his (Power's) horse outside the Seymour bank, as he proposed, while he went in and robbed it. He also stated that he once prevented Kelly from shooting a harmless traveller, on the road between Benalla and Mansfield, out of mere devilment.

But it must be remembered, in receiving and weighing these accusations, that Power was under the impression that he was "sold" by, and owed his capture to, Kelly, though a greater mistake never was made, for the man who pocketed the price of Power's wretched carcase lived but a short time to enjoy the reward of an approving conscience, backed up by the comparatively trifling but somewhat comforting accompaniment of a few hundred pounds sterling, Government money.

There is every reason to believe – in fact, we know – that Ned Kelly was for some time associated with Power in his predatory excursions, though the fellowship could not have proved a very remunerative one, for it is calculated that, while trading alone, the elder partner of the firm did not average £1 per week, clear.

About the end of 1869, or the beginning of 1870, some horses being suddenly missing from Mount Battery Station, near Mansfield, then owned by John. P. Rowe, and Power being abroad, the loss was at once set down to his agency, and accordingly a party, including two constables, was organized at the station, and the track of the stolen animals followed for some distance towards the head of the King River, where they were finally lost sight of. It is believed by many that at one time, the party being unpleasantly close to Power and his then mate, Ned Kelly, the latter proposed to surrender, and that the elder bushranger, threatened to blow his brains out if he attempted it. The subsequent and recent proceedings of Ned Kelly, however, could apparently give the lie to the story.

About this date, one day shortly after noon, two men, armed with guns, made their appearance of the highest verge of a rocky and nearly perpendicular declivity, nearly overhanging and within rifle shot of the Mount Battery homestead. On the alarm being given, Rowe turned out with a rifle, and a friend of his (who had been lunching at the house) with a smooth-bore loaded with ball, to take stock of the doubtful visitors, the shorter of whom, as far as distance would permit judging, answered the description of the then dreaded Power, but the other, who was tall, and at that time rather slight, defied recognition, while the wildest and most improbably conjectures were suggested as to his identity. This youth actually was Ned Kelly, though, for the matter of that, it is not now known for certain, except to a comparatively few, who either of the strangers was.

As soon as Rowe had taken a good look at the excursionists, who appeared to be carefully examining the house and grounds, he raised his rifle and let drive at them, without the formality of a challenge or salute of any kind, an example that was quickly followed by his friend, in the same reckless, and, as we consider, altogether lawless manner. The first shot missed them, and the second, as Sir Boyle Roche would have said, hit them in the same place, producing no further effect than inducing Kelly to raise his gun and take a steady aim at the two, but before any mischief ensued, Power threw up the muzzle of the gun, and persuaded him to retire without firing. They then quickly disappeared from the view of the Battery garrison, and, mounting their horses, which were secured hard by, rode off at full speed towards the King River, which they reached that evening, and rested at Power's gunyah, near Quin's Station, so as to baffle the pursuit which they anticipated, and which did take place, with the almost inevitable result in such cases.

There was a good deal of excitement about the affair for a day or two at Mansfield, which soon died out, but the general verdict was that Rowe was not justified in firing at men who, for all he knew, might have been nothing more than harmless travellers.

We must now return to the proceedings of the most prominent characters in our history, and follow them to their lurking places in the Wombat Ranges.

CHAPTER VIII

"Wherein of antres vast, and deserts idle,
Rough quarries, rocks, and hills whose heads touch heaven,
It was my hint to speak."
— Shakespeare

Immediately after the unfortunate fracas with the police near Greta, Dan Kelly deemed it imperative to betake himself to hiding, and was soon joined by his brother Edward, both of them knowing that the evidence of one constable would outweigh the combined testimony of those who took part in the disturbance. They did not, nevertheless, leave the colony, nor did they fail often to visit their home and friends, until they had learned the result of the trial of their mother and the others.

It was on receiving news of her conviction that they made use of threats of reprisals; and then, mindful of the reward placed on the head of one and the warrant out against the other, they judiciously confined their wanderings, for the most part, to the almost impenetrable natural fastnesses of the Wombat Ranges, which lie about 16 to 17 miles N. and N.E. of Mansfield, and form part of the vast extent of mountainous country, stretching in a north-westerly direction from the head of the King River. They also took the precaution to make their visit's to their friends, like those of angels, few and far between.

This vast tract occupies an area of many square miles, and the country is of an almost unimaginable impracticable nature, save to the few who have been accustomed to traverse its gloomy recesses since boyhood. The hills are steep, the woods pathless, and the gullies deep, dark, and winding; vast gorges, bounded by almost perpendicular ranges, surfaced with sharp and slippery shingles, monotonous in their outlines, and apparently of interminable extent, as well as ever recurring features, form a labyrinthine territory from the mazes of which the most experienced bushman might well despair of extricating himself. For, although the region is permeated sparsely by small streams and creeks, the difficulties attendant on following their courses continuously are almost insurmountable, from the precipitous and obstructed character of the sides in very many places, while the neighbourhood, for the most part, is covered with thick scrub, and encumbered frequently with huge rocks and enormous trunks of fallen trees; the impenetrability of the first being intensified by the interlacing of the Australian vine (so called).

There are also to be met with several vast and secluded caverns, so that, altogether, a more admirably adapted retreat for fugitives from the grasp of the law could not be conceived, provided the refugees were fortunate enough to have made arrangements with reliable and trustworthy friends for the due supply for such food as they would require, over and above meat, which the vicinity would plenteously afford, in the shape of wild cattle, wombat and wallaby.

The place is, however, open to one objection, from a strategetical point of view – namely in the matter of affording a rapid retreat, if necessary; and it is allowed, on all hands, that a good general, in choosing a position, should always take into consideration of being obliged to retire, and endeavour to arrange so that a retrograde movement, if indispensable, might be made with as little difficulty as possible, and, above all, with the greatest attainable rapidity, more especially in the face of overwhelming numbers.

For, although it would be possible for one acquainted with the locality to remain hidden in the bosom of the Wombat Ranges for years, still he might by some fatality be discovered – either betrayed by the greed of gold in someone to whom blood-money seemed as fair and lovely as riches from any other source, by his own carelessness, or by chance, in which case, although the scrub and vine curtain – provided he gained its shelter – might for a time hide him from the pursuer, yet it might probably prove advisable to take horse at once, and seek a temporary asylum elsewhere.

For such a race for life a good horse would be indispensable, and a corn-fed one at that; whereas the Wombat Ranges, near the best hiding places, are not sufficiently grassed to keep a horse even in fair, soft condition; and, besides, the appearance of a horse in the locality might lead to an unusually severe scrutiny of the surrounding neighbourhood.

Yet there is no doubt that the difficulty may, by some means, be got over, and most probably, indeed certainly, has been so by the Kelly gang, whose leader is too good a general to overlook the possibility of being sold, or, at least, an attempt being made in that direction, unless, indeed, the idea put forward had been true – that the gang had prepared a log fortress, victualled, properly loopholed, and cleared round of all shelter for besiegers, to which they could make their final retreat, and sell their lives as dearly as possible.

To this part of the country, then, the Kellys retired, with a view of avoiding the consequences of a charge which they professed to be unjust, and which is not generally believed to be, if not groundless, at least gravely exaggerated misstated.

Setting aside the horse-stealing charge, which has yet to be proved, and supposing, for the sake of argument, that, in the Fitzpatrick affair, the Kellys were more sinned against that sinning, what could be more natural than their seeking shelter from arrest, knowing the array they would have against them, and conscious that they would be powerless in the hands of their opponents?

There are hundreds, if not thousands, of good men and true in this colony alone who would infinitely prefer freedom, though purchased with such a wild, harassing and comfortless life as that of the Kelly gang must be, to imprisonment for the better part of their existence, under the ban of a crime of which they were innocent.

The circumstances of the case, though, whether the charge be true or otherwise, afford not the least excuse for the highly injudicious, not to say barbarous, course subsequently adopted by the band in regard to the police.

As was inferred previously, the refugees still occasionally visited and were visited by some of their more intimate friends, who, out of (illegal) kindness and sympathy, supplied them with rations, and information as to the movements of the police, as far as they could be ascertained. This was admitted on all hands to be extremely improper, reprehensible, and totally contrary to law; yet a few seemed to think, and still fewer ventured to say, that it was extremely natural for these misguided people to be ruled by their affections, regardless of public opinion, which guides most persons, and the majesty of the law, which awes a great number, and to persist in affording assistance to the wanderers, in defiance of both.

We refer here to the period of time during which the Kellys were charged with what, in comparison with their subsequent terrible acts, was a mere bagatelle; afterwards this sort of assistance was confined to those more near connections, who, while they condemned their conduct, could not be expected to utterly banish all human feelings of commiseration for the hunted outlaws.

Before long, Ned and Dan decided that they ought to adopt some means of recruiting their finances, which were down to zero, as they did not like being a drain of the resource of others; so, after taking a spell at fencing in the neighbourhood of the Merrijig, in a remote locality, bordering on, but to the south-east of their position, and some ten miles from their actual haunt, they made up their minds to try their fortune at gold digging in the heart of the mountains they had chosen for their retreat, where two parties of adventurous diggers had previously done reasonably well.

This seems to throw considerable doubt upon the report that they intention was to enter on a course of highway robbery through the country.

Accordingly, in company with two mates, named Joseph Byrne and Stephen Hart, they commenced digging – or, rather, sluicing operations on a small stream not very distant from the Stringy-bark Creek, which they persevered in for some time, with the ordinary fluctuations of luck incidental to that industry.

Sufficient gold, however, was obtained periodically, not only to procure the necessaries they required during the portion of their withdrawal from the busy world, but also to lay in supplies, which they – cached in various spots, with a view to future contingencies. They also constructed a good log hut near the site of their operations, which they fitted up with the ordinary conveniences of bush life, and carefully loopholed in case of an attack.

Of course the law, and the reward offered for Ned Kelly, demanded their pursuit and arrest; but it is sad to think that, had it been compatible with that law to ignore their existence during their voluntary exile, as it were, from civilization, and had the temptation of the glittering reward been removed, the sacrifice of three valuable lives, which plunged two families into unutterable grief, might have been avoided, and four wretched men might have escaped being involved in the crime of wilful and deliberate murder.

From the fact of Byrne and Hart (though they had been "in trouble" on some trifling charges on various occasions) not being actually "wanted" by the police at the time they went into partnership with the Kellys, it may justly be inferred that they did not join them with the design of anticipation of participating in any act whereby their liberties or lives might be jeopardized or forfeited. Indeed, it was though by some that their presence at the deplorable tragedy of the 26th October was accidental, or, at any rate, they had no prevision of the terrible ending of the bloody encounter.

Be it as it may, they are now as guilty in the eye of the inexorable law as though they had planed and executed the slaughter unaided and alone.

CHAPTER IX

"Oh, what a rash and bloody deed is this!"
– Hamlet

On or about Monday, the 21st of October, 1878, information was received by Ned Kelly and his mates that two parties of police were about to be despatched in pursuit of him and his brother, under the impression that they were camped near the head waters of the King, a favourite haunt of Power's, near which, under peculiar circumstances, he was taken prisoner, as before observed.

A council of was at once held, and it was at first proposed to retire to a more distant locality, temporarily, for safety; but finally it was decided to watch the movements of the police – a performance easy of accomplishment in that quarter – and, if opportunity offered, to "stick them up", giving them the option of surrender, which it was believed they would adopt, and, after depriving them of their horses, arms, ammunition, and rations, to handcuff them together, and suffer them to depart, after which performance it was intended by the band to retire to the Strathbogie Ranges, or such other secluded place as might seem safest and most convenient.

The information proved correct, for, in the early part of the same week, a party of police, under the command of Sergeant Strachan, started from Greta, and on Friday a detachment of four, led by Sergeant Kennedy, left Mansfield to achieve the capture of the Kellys. With the former body of men – the melancholy interest being centred on that sent out mention that on the day of the murder they were camped within four miles of Kennedy's party, and that had they followed along the spur which they were travelling in the early part of the day, instead of turning down to the right hand as they did, they would inevitably have formed a junction with the other detachment in time to have prevented the catastrophe which took place in the evening. Upon such apparently trifling circumstances do the most momentous events sometimes turn.

The Mansfield party started on horseback, with two pack-horses laden with a tent, a fortnight's provisions, blankets, and a large stock of ammunition; and they were armed, in addition to a revolver each, with a Spencer repeating rifle and a double-barrelled breach-loading fowling piece, which evidenced an anticipation of a determined resistance, and renders still more inexplicable the foolhardy conduct which will presently appear. It is stated – we know not on what grounds – that information of the departure of the police from Mansfield was at once carried across the bush to the Kellys by an emissary who was watching proceedings.

The party consisted of Sergeant Kennedy, of Mansfield; with Constables Scanlon, from Benalla; Lonigan, from Violet Town; and McIntyre, of Mansfield. At mid-day they camped for rest and refreshment, and in the afternoon reached Stringybark Creek in the Wombat Ranges, about 17 miles from their starting point and here they set up their tent, intending to reconnoitre for a day or two, and, if necessary, then shift towards the head of the King.

The spot where they established their halt was a small clearing on a rise alongside of the creek, near the ruins of two small huts, one of which was burnt down, and had been the temporary residence of three prospectors, named Reynolds, Bromfield and Lynch, who worked the creek for a short time with indifferent success.

The level space, though pretty well cleared, is surrounded by thick, heavy timber and scrub, and on the right hand side has a patch of very tall spear or sword-grass, which affords a jungle-like cover. In front of the tent, and between it and the creek, were two fallen trees, the ends being crossed at a right angle; there were also some stumps of trees that had been felled in the clearing.

The following morning, leaving McIntyre – whose turn it was to cook – and Lonigan in camp, Kennedy and Scanlan went out with the avowed intention of exploring the creek, opinions being divided as to whether they were on Holland's creek or a branch of the King, a fact that does not accurately dovetail with the statement that, knowing themselves to be 15 miles from the head of the King, they did not think they were near the Kellys, which is adduced as an excuse for venturing to divide the party, and the absurdity of McIntyre's leaving his revolver in the tent.

It rather tallies with an opinion that has been expressed by more than one – that there was no idea of the Kelly's having received a reinforcement; that they were suspected by Kennedy and Scanlan to be in the vicinity; and that these two went out with the desire to capture them without the interference or assistance of their fellow troopers. It is now too late to obtain any evidence as to the real facts, and speculation can lead to no definite result.

During the forenoon, McIntyre thought he heard a strange noise down the creek; so, taking the double-barrelled fowling piece and some cartridges, he forthwith proceeded to search for the cause, Lonergan remaining in solitary occupation of the camp. Seeing nothing unusual, McIntyre turned back, and on the way tested his skill as a marksman on a couple of parrots which he met. History does not record whether either or both fell to his gun, but it is stated that the unusual sound of the shots caught the quick ear of Ned Kelly, who at once jumped to the conclusion that they originated with some of those custodians of the peace whose close acquaintance he was unwilling to make, especially if he were taken at a disadvantage. Guided by the direction of the unwonted sound in those dreary solitudes, the gang were not long in discovering the whereabouts of the police, whom they rightly judged to be in pursuit of them, and were, doubtless, not only astonished but pleased to find that two of the party were absent. After some consultation not far from the camp they determined to carry out their resolution as to "bailing up" the constables; and, as there was now an opportunity of taking them by twos, no resistances or bloodshed was expected. Between four and five o'clock in the afternoon, the bushrangers – for they had not yet earned the title of highwaymen – silently creeping through the scrub, noticed McIntyre standing near a stump in front of, and about fifty yards from, the tent, where the billy was on a small fire. The constable had his back turned towards them, with Lonigan at his side. In the angle formed by the fallen trees before mentioned there was a large fire, which McIntyre, in anticipation of a raw, cold evening, had kindled. Creeping noiselessly through and almost to the verge of the patch of sword-grass in skirmishing order, but without supports, they suddenly, on a signal from their leader, who was on the right of the line, simultaneously pointed their guns at the constables, Ned calling out in a loud and commanding tone, "Bail up, throw your arms up!" – an order that was reiterated by all the crew. Dan Kelly came next to his brother in the line, with Byrne and Hart next.

On hearing the voices, McIntyre turned sharply round, and seeing himself covered by four guns, while he was totally unarmed, he immediately and wisely obeyed, and threw up his hands. He had left his revolver in the tent while attending to the cooking, but it would not have been any better if he had it on him; on the contrary, it might have led to his death, as in the case of Lonigan, who attempted to gain the shelter of a tree, at the same time trying to draw his revolver, when Ned Kelly fired a charge of small bullets at him, one of which, entering his brain, through the orbit of the right eye, brought him to the ground a corpse; and as he was struck, he cried out, "Oh, Christ! I'm shot!" Instinct and force of habit, not reason, must have prompted to put his hand to his revolver, for the bravest man need not have blushed to surrender in the face of such odds. The other wounds from the scattered pellets were comparatively unimportant.

If the following tale, which has been going the rounds, has any foundation in fact – and it's credited by many persons in Benalla and elsewhere, though Kelly has, as yet, been silent on the subject, and he is not a man who loves much cross questioning, though he freely volunteers information – there would seem to be a strange fatality in the misfortune which overtook Lonigan on this sad occasion.

It is said that Ned Kelly, a few years since, being on a spree in Benalla, was one evening rather disorderly and noisy, whereupon three constables, one being Lonigan, attempted to arrest him. Kelly, however, placing his back to a wall, set them at defiance, knocking them down like ninepins as fast as they came up. An acquaintance, a butcher, happening to be passing, and taking in the situation at a glance, sensibly recommended Kelly to go with the police quietly, or the affair might take a more serious turn for him. He at once said he would let the friend "snap the handcuffs on him", but swore he would never let the police have the satisfaction of doing so. The irons being adjusted on these conditions, Kelly went quietly with the constables towards the lock-up; but the story goes on to say, the police, when they got him safe out of sight on the road, commenced to handle him very roughly, and at last knocked him down. The most improbable part of the tale, though within the bounds of credibility, comes last – namely, that while he lay on the ground manacled, Lonigan deliberately jumped on him, breaking three of his ribs, which caused him to be laid up for nine months. It is further said, that after Kelly was thus maltreated (if he was so), he exclaimed, "Well, Lonigan, I never shot a man yet; but if ever I do, so help me G—, you will be the first!"

As a matter of fact, Kelly did not recognize Lonigan at the time of the murders, so that his presence and death amounted to merely a coincidence if the charge against him were true. It is a remarkable fact that, when leaving Violet Town to join in the pursuit of the Kellys, Lonigan returned twice a considerable distance to bid his family farewell; and moreover, declared that he knew he would not return alive from the expedition. This would seem as if he had a forecasting of his fate in case of meeting the bushrangers.

Scanlon, too, appeared to have gloomy forebodings, though a brave and fearless man, for he called out to the wardsman of the local hospital, "I may never come back, and, if so, you can take my dog", an animal upon which he set great value.

But to return to the scene. The four bushrangers, when Lonigan fell, rushed forward towards McIntyre, ordering him to keep his hands up still, and asked him if he had any firearms. When he replied in the negative, they inquired where his revolver was, to which he answered, "In the tent," upon which Ned Kelly, after carefully searching him, told him he might drop his hands, as he had no arms. The party then took Lonigan's revolver from his belt, about which there was some dispute as to who should retain it, and secured McIntyre's, a double-barrelled breach-loader, which a minister of the gospel had kindly lent, and a quantity of ammunition, which were in the tent. When this operation was satisfactorily completed, Ned Kelly, looking towards the body of Lonigan, said, with an expression and tone of genuine regret, "Dear, dear, what a pity the fool tried to get away; but you're all right" (to McIntyre). A due consideration of this fact, which is corroborated by McIntyre's sworn evidence, would favour the supposition that there was no original design to shoot the police.

The gang then indulged in some tea and a smoke, forcing McIntyre to partake of the refreshment first, as a guarantee that no trap had been laid for them in the shape of poison or narcotics; it having been pretty broadly asserted, and in some quarters believed, that the deep sleep during which Power was arrested was brought about by means of which is commonly known as "hocussing"; in fact, that he owed his capture chiefly to the seductive charms of a bottle of brandy, behind the Delilah-like smiles of which there lurked a powerful but unsuspected soporific. This rumour, true or false, had the effect of putting the Kellys on their guard; so that they were not, and are not, likely to be caught in a similar snare. After the light repast, Dan Kelly, producing a pair of regulation handcuffs – Lonigan's – suggested their application to McIntyre; but Ned, significantly tapping his gun, which he had carefully reloaded, said, "No, there's something better than handcuffs here", adding, to McIntyre, "don't you try to get away, for if you do, I'll track you to Mansfield, if necessary, and shoot you at the very police station".

He then asked his prisoner when he expected his mates to return, and was told that he did not know, as they had already stayed out longer than he had anticipated, so he expected they were bushed. After a host of questions had been put and answered as to the horses and equipment of the party &c., Ned Kelly asked where the repeating rifle was, and when he learned that the party out patrolling had it with them, inquired their names. When he was told, he remarked that he had never heard about Kennedy, but believed, by all accounts, that Scanlon was a flash - ; than which he never made a greater mistake, for Scanlon was as fine a fellow of his kind as ever breathed.

In this we see grounds for the refutation of another of those untenable assertions so freely circulated in relation to the deplorable events which happened on October the 26th - namely (while speculation was rife as to the probable fate of Kennedy), that the Kellys would torture and kill him because he was known to be so active and energetic in the pursuit and prosecution of cattle and sheep-stealers. In the course of the further colloquy relating to the absent men, McIntyre asked Kelly what his intentions were with regard to them, expressing a hope, at the same time, that he would not shoot them, adding most emphatically that he (McIntyre) would a thousand times rather be shot than be the means of leading his comrades to destruction, the more so that one of them was the father of a large family. Kelly indignantly said, "I'm no coward; I'll shoot no man if he'll hold up his hands and surrender".

To a question from McIntyre as to whether he intended to shoot him, the reply was as reasonable as it was ready - "No, what would I shoot you for? I could have done that half an hour ago if I liked", adding the supplementary remark, "At first I thought you were Constable Flood, and if you were, we'd have roasted you on that fire", pointing to the blazing pile which flamed and crackled in the angle of the two fallen trees. It might be safely affirmed, though he says nothing about it, that McIntyre blessed his stars that he was not Flood on that occasion, whose unpleasant relations with the Kellys, it has been hinted, did not originate in any matter of police duty owing to a breach of law by the Kellys, but rather to a disturbance of the domestic peace of the family, caused by a breach of the moral law, which would warrant the utmost indignation on the part of the brothers, as having suffered a social injury, which, in the days of duelling, would have only admitted of one remedy, and that but a partial one at the best. Soon after the conversation just detailed, Kelly directed his mates to conceal themselves, and wait the coming of Kennedy and Scanlon, which they did; Dan and Steve retreating into the speargrass and scrub, while Byrne found an ambush in the tent.

At this time Kelly was standing near the fire, keeping McIntyre close to him as before. He then went on to tell him what, perhaps, he may have heard before – namely that Fitzpatrick was the cause of his turning out, and that his mother, Skillion and Williamson were convicted on false evidence; that they no more had revolvers in their hands when the outrage was supposed to have been committed than he (McIntyre) had at that moment; and, further, that at the time, he (Kelly) was not within miles of the place. Having elicited from McIntyre that the "Sydney man" who shot Sergeant Wallings in New South Wales was, in his turn, shot by the police, Kelly said, "And I suppose you ——s have come out here to shoot us?" to which McIntyre returned, "No, we have come to apprehend you," on which Kelly, with a look of contempt, said, "Isn't it a shame to see fine, big, strapping looking men like you in a lazy, loafing billet like the police force? Now, if I let you go, you will have to leave it". This McIntyre faithfully (and judiciously) promised to do, at the same time neglecting to specify the precise date upon which it was his intention to tender his resignation to the Chief Commissioner of Police.

The arrested constable then proceeded to pump his captor as to what his intentions were, in the event of his (McIntyre's) being able to persuade his comrades to surrender; but he only succeeded in eliciting the ambiguous and anything but reassuring reply, "You had better get them to surrender, for if they escape I will shoot you; or if you let them know in any way that we are here, you will be shot down at once; but if you get them to surrender, I will let you go in the morning. We will handcuff you all night, as we intend sleeping here, and we want a sleep badly". Kelly afterwards afforded him an equally unsatisfactory promise – unsatisfactory because, although the bushranger pledged himself conditionally not to harm the three survivors, yet the undertaking lost much of the value in consequence of a contingency with which it was hampered; for, notwithstanding the leader promised faithfully not to shoot the police if they surrendered, when asked whether he would prevent the others of the gang from doing so, he said, "They can please themselves". This was probably interpreted by the prisoner to mean than it was 3 to 1 they would be all killed – by no means a soothing reflection for a man in his critical position.

Portraits of Kennedy and Scanlon

CHAPTER X

"If it be aught toward the general good,
Set honour in one eye and death i' the other,
And I will look on both indifferently;
For, let the gods so speed me as I love
The name of honour more than I fear death."
— Julius Caesar

At this stage of the proceedings, and before there was an opportunity of consulting the other bushrangers as to their views on the subject under consideration, the horse-tramp of the absent constables heralded their approach, and almost simultaneously they came in sight, near the border of the clearing on the side of the space opposite the clump of speargrass, and rather to one side of the tent. Kelly, on noticing this exclaimed, "Hush, lads, here they come!" and ordered McIntyre to sit down on one of the crossed logs, at the same time ensconsing himself behind it close by, with an unmistakable hint that disobedience would be followed by a rifle ball through the body. McIntyre thereupon said earnestly in a low tone, "Oh, Kelly, for God's sake don't shoot the men, and I will get them to surrender!"

Following the colloquy – if it may be so called – between the constable and Kelly, Kennedy unsuspiciously advanced into the clearing, having Scanlon a couple of horses' length in his rear; and McIntyre going forward, told him quietly that they were surrounded by Kelly and his party, advising him, under the circumstances, to surrender. Immediately, at a sign from Ned Kelly, the police were covered by the guns of the gang, with the command of "Bail up! Throw up your hands!"

Kennedy, thinking it is presumed, that the whole was a lark of Lonigan's, smilingly placed his hand on his revolver case, whereupon shots were instantly fired by some of the bushrangers. Both Kennedy and Scanlon then hurriedly dismounted, and the latter struck for a tree some three or four yards distant, endeavouring the while to unsling the Spencer rifle which hung at his back, as he ran; but before he could gain the friendly shelter, or disengage the piece, he fell from a bullet which struck him in the side, under the right arm, the blood spurting instantaneously from the wound. Some shots were then fired by the Kelly party, but without effect, which is the more strange in that some of the guns were loaded with a number of small bullets – a course which accounts for the numerous wounds found afterwards on the bodies of the dead, although so few shots were fired after this stage of the proceedings.

After several fruitless attempts apparently to draw his revolver, Kennedy, recognizing the futility of resistance, surrendered, calling out, "All right, boys – all right; don't shoot – don't shoot!" And the case must have seemed truly hopeless to induce a man of Kennedy's well-known pluck and daring to "cave-in"; indeed, if the source from which the account of his final struggle with his antagonists may be relied on, he was possessed of an indomitable courage – SECOND TO NONE.

Presently, however, Kennedy managed to suddenly extricate his revolver from the case, and at once opened fire on his attackers, whereupon McIntyre, being defenceless, unable to render any aid, and concluding correctly that Kennedy's breach of parol, as it were, after surrendering, would draw down the vengeance of the band, and consequently, by affording the excuse of broken conditions, eventuate in the slaughter of all, very wisely jumped on the horse nearest to him, which was Kennedy's, and which Kennedy showed no intention of reaching, and galloped off. His adventures and escapes must be postponed to form the subject of a future chapter, while we follow the fortunes of the ill-starred sergeant to the bitter end.

Many persons, since the publication of the particulars attending the melancholy episode which occupies this portion of our narrative, have rashly and hastily stigmatized Constable McIntyre as a coward; but a careful consideration of the details and surroundings will go far to establish the belief that although he may be physically timid (and many brave men have been and are so), yet the charge of cowardice, in its true meaning, is one that can never be brought home to him.

In the midst of the fearful circumstances which surrounded him, in the hands of men whom he looked upon as faithless, unscrupulous, and bloodthirsty scoundrels, with the terrible fate of one of his comrades before his eyes, and the possibility of a similar one being in store for himself, he never lost his coolness, nor did he exhibit any undue or selfish anxiety to secure his own safety. On the contrary, his chief energies appear to have been devoted to the preservation of his absent comrades from injury, for which end he used the sole means at his command – persuasion; for, being without any weapon, he could do no more.

The worst accusation that can be brought against him is that of fool-hardy carelessness in allowing himself to be surprised without arms, in the centre of a country occupied by well-armed, courageous and determined enemies.

The separation of the detachment was, in itself, an act of supreme folly, especially in a locality where nature had, apparently, lent her utmost powers and ingenuity to affording every facility for ambush, espial, and surprise to any who, acquainted with the pathless solitudes of the place, might be objects of attack to a party ignorant of its minutest, to say nothing of its general, topography.

CHAPTER XI

"The tyrannous and bloody act is done,
The most arch deed of piteous massacre."

As soon as Kennedy commenced shooting, the bushrangers took to cover among the timber, merely showing themselves partially from time to time, with a view to draw his fire and induce him to exhaust his ammunition in unavailing efforts to hit them. During his noble defence, until he had emptied five chambers of his revolver, without any damage to his assailants, he stood boldly up, scarcely changing from his original position, not throwing away his cartridges recklessly, but taking cool and deliberate aim on each occasion, one of his balls passing through Ned Kelly's whiskers, and another through his sleeve, but with no other result. A shot was then fired by one of the gang without any apparent effect, when Kennedy instantly commenced retreating, at a rapid pace, through the bush in a direction at a slight angle to that taken by McIntyre in his flight, the Kellys following in hot pursuit. After running some thirty chains, and perceiving, from the proximity and rapidly decreasing distance of his pursuers, that he was cut off from the possibility of escape, and that all was lost but honour, Kennedy, as a last resource, darted behind a large tree, as as soon as the elder Kelly came within pistol range, played his last card by discharging at him the sole remaining shot in his pistol from behind the timber screen. But although the weapon was levelled with a true eye and steady hand, the bullet failed to strike the living mark for which it was so sincerely intended; for Kelly, noticing that the barrel was pointed directly at his head, quick as thought dropped to his knees, yet only just in time, for, as he fell, he distinctly heard the "ping" of Kennedy's bullet passing harmlessly through that part of the space so lately filled and rapidly vacated by the upper portion of his stalwart frame.

Springing up quickly, he at once returned the fire from his gun, with fatal precision, the ball entering Kennedy's right side, who fell, mortally wounded, and fighting to the last like a true hero, as he was, close to the tree, where his body was eventually discovered by a search party from Mansfield.

It appears that a motion of Kennedy's arm; indicative, apparently, of an intention to fire again, supplied the motive for shooting to Kelly, who was not aware that all the chambers of the revolver had been emptied.

In a short time Hart and Byrne were observed approaching the spot; but when they saw Kennedy down and in the custody of their mates, they hurried off with the double object of chasing McIntyre, who, as detailed before, had fled from the scene of action, and carrying out some orders previously given.

Helpless, and suffering intense agony from his wound, the victim lay passively on the spot where he fell, and presently the victors touched by his noble and persistent defence against the over-whelming odds which combined the comparatively large number of his assailants, the quantity of their arms, and the limited number of shots at his command, commenced to do what they could, though that was but little, to alleviate his sufferings. The elder altered the wounded man's position from time to time, as required, so as to afford him what relief was possible, while the younger hurried to the creek for water to cool and moisten his parched and clammy lips.

As may be anticipated, the two bushrangers took this opportunity to try and extract from the dying man as much information as possible of various matters which were of interest and importance to themselves, and which they were not likely to gather from any other source. About an hour and a half was expended in this attempt, but the knowledge gained was not of such extent or so much value as they looked forward to.

Meagre as it was, though, it would be highly injudicious to give it publicity.

But loyal reticence was not the only cause of the failure to elicit the desired particulars from Michael Kennedy; its origin was to be traced to a still more admirable source – namely, the domestic affections of that true-hearted man, who, feeling his end drawing near, had turned his thoughts entirely to the dear wife and little ones he had left at home, then little dreaming of the dreadful catastrophe that was to make them, the one a sorrowing widow, and the others orphans depending on her unaided care.

During the time that preceded his death, he, on every possible occasion, diverted the channel of conversation into the direction of his home.

He repeatedly spoke, in the most affectionate and regretful terms, of Mrs. Kennedy and his children, not unfrequently making reference to the infant son that had been snatched from him by death not long before, thus sustaining the character he was always known, in his private life, to deserve and bear, of a fond husband and doting father, in whose thoughts the welfare and happiness of his idolized family were paramount to all earthly considerations; and it is a pleasure to be able to record that an example reciprocation of his well-bestowed affections ever rewarded his tender care.

The Kellys would have been less than human had they not been painfully penetrated by such a heart-rending scene. It would have taken more hardened offenders to look with indifference on the spectacle brought about by their act, of the brave strong man stretched at their feet, struggling in his last agony, amid the deepening gloom of that dismal forest, his indomitable mind unselfishly filled with sorrow, anxiety, and the most dismal forebodings for his nearest and dearest, doomed, in this world, never to hear his welcome voice again.

To such an extent was Edward Kelly touched at last, that he cried out excitedly, and with a genuine impulse of remorse, "Well, Kennedy, I am sorry that I shot you, for you're a brave man. Here, take my gun and shoot me", to which the dying man, with true greatness of soul, replied, "No, I forgive you from my heart, and I pray that God may forgive you too".

After a few minutes' talk, chiefly devoted to expression of regret on the part of the Kellys, and requests by Kennedy to drop the subject as unavailing, the latter, being propped up at his request, and being handed a rough note-book and pencil from his pocket, proceeded to write on some loose sheets certain memoranda, consisting chiefly of an outline of his then pitiful condition, and advice as to his wife's future proceedings, together with his good wishes and farewells. He continued writing for some little time – in fact, until his rapidly-waning strength obliged him to desist; and he then delivered the papers into Ned Kelly's charge, with an earnest request that he would, if possible, cause it to be conveyed to Mrs. Kennedy's hands – a request that Kelly promised faithfully to comply with, if ever a favourable opportunity should occur.

This pledge seemed to have a soothing effect on the sergeant's mind, but the pain was evidently becoming more and more insupportable every moment, and soon his brain seemed to wander, by fits and starts, as evidenced by incoherent mutterings.

By this time, which was roughly estimated at about seven o'clock, it was, from prudential motives too obvious to need recital, deemed advisable by the gang to prepare for a speedy departure, but Kelly could not bear the horrible idea of leaving the wounded man to die alone, in such lingering anguish, both of mind and body; therefore, seizing a moment when he thought the wandering fit was on, and vacancy in the sergeant's gaze, he endeavoured to place a shot gun (the breach-loader) in a position to enable him to put a speedy period to his existence. Kennedy, however, was not so far insensible as not to notice the action and interpret its meaning, for he exclaimed, though with considerable difficulty, and many interruptions, "Let me alone, for God's sake – let me live, if I can, for the sake of my poor wife and family; surely you have shed enough blood already". Without waiting to hear any more painful remonstrances, or allowing himself time for reflection, Kelly then, nerving himself, by an effort, for the dreadful deed, placed the muzzle of the gun to the victim's left breast, and fired the shot which closed the brave men's career. He died instantaneously, without a struggle and without a groan.

Kelly might have exclaimed, with Othello –

"I, that am cruel, am yet merciful;

I would not have thee linger in thy pain".

The Kellys then turned out the dead man's pockets, retaining all that was worth securing, including a valuable gold watch, a small sum of money, and two excellent photographs of themselves. A small pocket-knife escaped search by having slipped through a hole in a waistcoat pocket and lodged in the lining, and was found in the clothes of the deceased of the morgue. The report that the corpse was mutilated by the cutting off of an ear, is, like many other rumours in connection with the affair, altogether without foundation. On the contrary, the Kellys were full of admiration at the bravery of the deceased, in recognition of which they laid him out, and covered him carefully up in his regulation cloak, which they went to the tent for on purpose. And thus he was found by the search party, as

"He lay like a warrior taking his rest,

with his martial cloak around him."

Police find the body of Mr Kennedy

CHAPTER XII

"What can his friend 'gainst thronging numbers dare?
Ah, must he rush, his comrade's fate to share?"
The Episode of Nisus and Euryalus

When McIntyre, despairing of affording any aid to Kennedy, even by the sacrifice of his own life, spring on the horse, the animal, probably either confused by the unaccustomed noise of firing, or knowing that he was bestridden by a stranger, stood stock still for a moment, regardless of the rider's heels, but presently made a plunge forward, which caused him to lose hold on one stirrup, and while he leaned over one side to recover it, the outlaws, although they had not fired on him personally, set up a wild cheer, either of triumph, under the impression that he was wounded, or derision at his precipitate flight - possibly a mixture of both. Steering due west, by the guidance of the sun, he dashed at full gallop down the creek, and urging the horse to its utmost speed, by means of a small branch which he had snatched in passing, never shirking any obstacle on the ground that threatened to impede his progress, and miraculously escaping, by instinctively avoiding, the trunks and overhanging limbs that otherwise would have shattered his limbs or swept him from the saddle, while crashing through the, luckily, dry and withered scrub, that reduced his clothing to tatters and covered him with cuts and bruises, he succeeded in holding his way, otherwise in safety, for the space of about half a mile.

At this point, his horse, either tripping over some impediment or slipping on a rock, came down heavily, flinging the rider on the ground half stunned.

Rapidly recovering, however, and finding that, fortunately, no bones were broken, he got up, and seeing that the noble animal, which had been his preserver so far, was too much exhausted for further reliance to be placed on its efforts, he determined to continue his flight on foot.

In order, then, that the horse, if found by any of the gang, who he firmly believed were in pursuit of him, should not be recognized, and thus give the clue to the direction he was following, he took off the saddle, which he "planted" in an adjacent log; then, heading the animal towards the south, and removing the bridle, he struck it therewith sharply on the buttocks, which sent it off, at a smart pace, in a course at right angles to the one he had decided on adhering to.

After travelling half or three–quarters of a mile further, as rapidly as his injuries and the antagonistic nature of the ground would permit, at the same time with due regard to the avoidance of making any noise that might prate of his whereabouts, he reached the head of a gully leading down to a stream called Holland's Creek, which is a confluent of the Broken River, entering it on the eastern side, at the township of Benalla. Here he set about finding some secure hiding-place where he might secrete himself until darkness set in, judging that his retreat would be conducted more safely under the friendly cover of night. His first selection was a hollow tree, but considering not only that the amount of shelter was insufficient, but that it would be a likely place to invite search, he rejected it in favour of a large wombat hole. Into this orifice he manager, painfully, to insert himself, feet foremost some three yards, when the narrowing of the cavity forbade his further entrance, while at the same time the limited circumference of the foremost part of the hollow afforded insufficient space to admit of his breathing freely, owing to the compression of his chest. After submitting to this uncomfortable state of affairs for about a quarter of an hour, and his hearing, sharpened to the utmost by painful apprehensions, giving no hint of any unwelcome intruders on his solitude, he cautiously emerged beyond the mouth of his hiding place, and wrote on a page of his note-book a memorandum, of which the following is a verbatim copy:–

"Ned Kelly, Dan and two others stuck us up while we were unarmed. Lonigan and Scanlon are shot. I am hiding in a wombat hole until dark. The Lord have mercy on me. Scanlon tried to get his gun out". He wrote this with the intention of leaving it in his hole of refuge, in view of the possibility of his being captured, searched, and probably slaughtered by the gang, and in the vague hope that, should such an event occur, the written statement might be discovered and furnish the clue to the murderers. McIntyre states that, at the time, he feared that the gang would, either by burning him in the hole, or some other torturing process, put him to death. If, however, history repeats itself, as it is said to do, the fate dreaded by the constable would have befallen the chief of the gang.

Making all allowance for the excitement caused by the fearful position in which McIntyre found himself, we can scarcely compliment him either on the candour exhibited in his memo, or the ingenuity displayed in the choice of its hiding place; for, in the first place, the only one of the police unarmed, at the time of the attack, was himself; and, in the next, if the murderers put him to death by the absurdly improbable process of burning in the hole, the note-book would inevitably perish with him; and, finally, if they pulled him out of the hole and killed him, they would to a certainty search the place, and even if not, what chance would there be of the book coming in the proper hands?

Having completed the entry in his note-book, he resumed his position in the burrow, and waited patiently the advent of darkness, which did not set in for some two hours, after the lapse of which, prudence and necessity urging him to continue his homeward journey, he evacuated the premises he had so uncomfortably occupied.

When lying – we cannot say resting - in his cramped hiding place, which faced the setting sun, he had specially noted "a bright particular star", which he determined to use as a guide on his homeward march, and, acting upon this resolution, was led down the gully towards Holland's Creek. But conceiving that if he walked in his stocking feet he would not make so much noise as if shod, he divested himself of his boots, and reaching the stream, crossed it on his hands and knees, as a further means of baffling the pursuers, who he dreaded were at his heels; then, ascending some rising ground, he lay down, exhausted, to rest. Gaining confidence from the absence of any indications of pursuit, and feeling extremely foot-sore, he resumed his boots,

"Which his nimble haste
Had falsely thrust upon contrary feet"

a fact by which it is attempted to prove – we know not how – that determination gave him strength.

When he had travelled a couple of miles or so further, he lost the run of his guiding star, and was obliged to fall back upon a pocket-compass he had with him.

To consult this was a doubtful, dangerous alternative; for, in the first place, he had only three matches, and in the next it involved the risk of being discovered by means of the light which it was necessary to strike. However, using his coat as a screen round his head, and looking, we presume, like a photographer focussing an object, he succeeded in lighting his second match (having dropped and lost his first), and dis-covered, to his satisfaction and slight surprise, he had been keeping his original course – west. Up to this point, he had been as successful as Barney O'Reardon, the navigator, wid his nor-aist coorse; but presently the country opposed such an aggregation of rough and otherwise insur-moutable features to his further progress, that he was constrained to strike southward, which, although it led him in a more direct line from that point to Mansfield, it also increased his likelihood of falling in with the gang, if still in search of him.

From this he was only able to pursue his journey by the aid of frequent intervals of rest, one of which, and almost the last, took place on the bank of the Blue Range Creek, which flows through Dueran Run, and empties itself into the Broken River, about eight miles from Mansfield as the crow flies.

When he reached this stream, which he mistook for Bridge's Creek, three miles to the eastward of it, but about equidistant from the township, hunger, weariness, excitement and pain had superinduced such a state of depression that he despaired of ever reaching Mansfield again.

Under this gloomy impression he wrote in his note-book – "I have been travelling all night, and am very weary. Nine a.m. Sunday. – I am lying on the edge of the creek named Bridge's."

At length, refreshed by a protracted response, he once more addressed himself to his journey and, after a toilsome and tedious struggle, he managed to totter into the farm-house of Mr. John McColl, distant about a mile and half from the township, at three o'clock in the afternoon.

The horror-stricken and sympathizing inmates, on hearing his story, and seeing the wounds and torn clothing, which showed his tale was a reality, at once set to work to relieve and comfort him to the best of their ability; but, being in a highly feverish state, he was unable to avail himself of the refreshments set before him to more than a very trifling extent.

In the meantime, in less than a quarter of an hour after his arrival, the thoughtful promptitude of the McColls had procured a buggy and horse, which were readily lent by a neighbouring farmer (Mr. Byrne), and in which McIntyre was speedily driven to the police camp by a member of the family, where he lost no time in giving, as accurately as his high state of nervous perturbation would allow, the details of the dreadful occurrences to Sub-Inspector Pewtress who, without a moment's delay, proceeded to organize a party to find the murdered constables, and search for Sergeant Kennedy, whose fate, at the time, was a subject of doubt and speculation to all but the gang of bushrangers.

The state of nervous excitement exhibited by McIntyre, at the termination of his sauve qui peut flight, can readily be understood.

A frantic effort on the part of an unarmed, defenceless fugitive to escape, at full speed, the clutches of four determined pursuers (as he thought), with the certainty that capture meant death, coupled with the fact of the flight taking place chiefly at night, over rough, rocky, wooded and unknown ranges, would not be likely to steady the nerves of the bravest man; and when, in addition to this, we reflect that the retreat through thick scrub and timber, which almost reduced the fugitive to a mass of cuts and bruises, we surely cannot view, with either surprise or contempt, the trepidation evinced by him after his race for life; while his return to the scene, as will be shown hereafter, on the self-same day, as guide to the search party, ought fully to exonerate him from any imputation of poltroonery which, through ignorance, thoughtlessness, or any other cause, may have been cast at him.

"He jests at scars that never felt a wound."

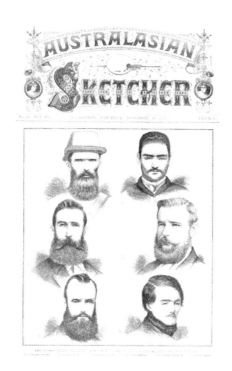

CHAPTER XIII

"They followed through toothed briars,
Sharp furzes, prickling goss, and thorns."
– Shakespeare

As has been already stated, Byrne and Hart, when they saw Kennedy at the mercy of their mates, started at once in pursuit of McIntyre whom they possibly regarded as an easy prey, under the impression that he was wounded.

But, as the reader is aware, they were mistaken in their supposition; so, after a comparatively brief and hurried search on foot, they hastened to where the horses of the gang, saddled, bridled, and with their swags fastened on, were secured, and, mounting their own cattle, galloped off, in pursuance of a previous arrangement, which will presently be understood, at the same time keeping an eye out for the missing constable.

After Kennedy's death, the Kellys returned to the camping place of the police, and, after emptying the pockets of the dead troopers to the tune of some £15, and a silver watch with guard, as well as securing Scanlon's revolver, repeating rifle, and finger ring, they proceeded to investigate the interior of the tent. Here they found and packed up the remaining rations and cartridges, with some blankets; and, heaping the unneeded articles and tent together, fired the pile, which was speedily reduced to ashes. While the burning was in progress they were startled by the explosion of two cartridges which had escaped their notice in the tent; but quickly guessing the cause of the reports, they took they way to where the remaining horses were tied, and, returning they loaded them with the spoils they had acquired.

Taking a farewell glance at the scene of the tragedy, they started for their hut, in the vicinity of the site of their digging operations, conversing as they went, in low tones, on the days proceedings. The greater part of their talk was tinged with a regret, that, what they deemed a stern necessity, had forced them to the murderous acts they had perpetrated, while the uncertainty that hung over McIntyre's escape did not tend to elevate their spirits by any means.

A desultory chat followed, which had reference to certain future movements, and this brought them to their temporary home, when, after dismounting, and bringing their plunder into the hut, they unsaddled the animals and secured them in the usual feeding place, not far from the dwelling. They then re-entered the hut, and, after making free with the stores taken from the police to satisfy their appetites, they retired to rest, and soon were wrapped in an sound and peaceful a slumber as though they had been sleeping the sleep of the just.

During this time Byrne and Hart were travelling, as fast as the darkness allowed, in most the same direction as that taken by McIntyre at first; but the fact of their gradually diverging to the north-westward will account of their not overtaking him. Another thing in his favour was, that the bushrangers did not stop to listen, or make any observations on their way, but kept pushing along as fast as circumstances and their acquaintance with the country allowed them.

Reaching the vicinity of the Broken River, after many hair-breadth escapes, from the irregularities of the surface and impending branches, they obtained refreshment and a relay of horses, and after a hasty meal, and leaving Hart to give an outline of what had happened, for the information of their entertainer (who dared not, if he wished, refuse to accommodate them), Byrne galloped off towards the Strathbogie ranges, in which neighbourhood he wanted to make some arrangements with a friend.

Crossing the Broken River and the telegraph line about four miles to the south of Barjarg Station homestead, in west-ward direction, he rode up the ascents near and above the source of the Glen Creek, and thence reached the tableland gold-diggings at the head of Brankeet Creek, and near the Hell's Hole and Dry Creeks, at about nine o'clock, having covered more than twenty miles in his ride. Here he called at a store to get a drink, and startled the proprietor by asking if he had heard about two constables having been shot in the Wombat ranges. He then rode on, and, as far as the public were concerned, all traces of him were lost, but crossing portions of the Junction and Borodomain runs, he made a detour which brought him to the destination he aimed at, about midnight.

Hart, on the other hand, took a north-easterly course, and headed for Greta, in the neighbourhood of which he arrived about two o'clock about following morning after a journey of at least 44 miles. Here Hart also made sundry arrangements, in view of possible contingencies, and narrated the particulars of the meeting with the police. It is true he could have saved ten or twelve miles by taking a more northerly course from the Wombat, but there were imperative reasons why he should visit the Broken River in company with Byrne. In all this, the men were simply carrying out the orders of their chief, upon whose foresight and intelligence they placed implicit reliance.

On Sunday night the two Kellys, who were naturally on the look out for an invasion of their stronghold, if not in pursuit of themselves, in quest of their victims, caught the sound of the search party approaching, as they were patrolling in the direction from which they expected them to arrive. After taking stock of them from a very short distance indeed, as well as could be in the gloom, they set out for Greta, and a little after daybreak on Monday camped in a secluded spot some six or seven miles to the south of it. They remained there quietly until after nightfall, when they concluded their journey at the house they were bound for, where they met Hart and also Byrne, who had returned from Strathbogie in the interim, according to orders. Having completed the business to which their visit was due, they set out, on fresh horses, for the mountain fastnesses they had come from, and which formed the safest retreat for them in such critical circumstances.

Being urged, for prudential motives, to deviate sometimes considerably from the direct route, and occasionally secrete themselves for a time, while one of them reconnoitred, they did not gain their haven of refuge until past midnight on the following Wednesday.

Previous to leaving the Wombat, the Kellys had removed almost all the stores from their hut to a place of safety altogether screened from observation, both by position and other advantages, which demands description. It was, in fact, a natural cellar, and was known to the gang as "the horseshoe", on account of its peculiar shape. It consisted of a

"Wondrous cave,

Whose sinuous windings in the mountain's breast

found double vent"

and was shaped like the letter U placed horizontally, thus ∩, only that one leg was shorter than the other. It was situated about midway up the side of a lofty, precipitous and rocky spur, surrounded, and, where mature permitted, clothed with the closest kind of scrub. The upper opening, which belonged to the shorter branch, was just within a belt of the before-mentioned scrub, while the lower one was in the bare face of the declivity, the former penetrating the hill to a distance of about ten or eleven yards before it took the downward bend connecting it with the latter, which extended into the ground for a length of forty-five feet or thereabouts.

There was an interval of about ten yards between these entrances, which was broken midway by a widely projecting ledge or rock – a reef – that crossed it and extended a long distance, in a slightly diagonal direction.

The upper leg, as we may term it, of this cavity was arched at the top, and of nearly equal dimensions as to the height and breadth at the bottom – that is to say, about five feet; and the proportions were continued on an average as far as half through the descending portion, where they suddenly narrowed to about eighteen inches, a measure which increased gradually towards the lower opening to three feet. The passage here assumed a flattened shape, not being much more than one foot across, though three feet high. The strait, as it were, between the two halves of the cavity was blocked by a rough mass of rock, which, admitting of ventilation and drainage, prevented any of the articles stowed away from falling through into the lower division, from which it would be difficult, perhaps impossible, to recover them.

Kelly's shack near Stringybark Creek

CHAPTER XIV

"And let the horsemen skirre the country round."
- Shakespeare

The township of Mansfield being the first place to which official intimation of the murders was conveyed, we will now glance at the events which originated and happened there during the time occupied by the foregoing circumstances.

When the shocking intelligence of the murder of Scanlon and Lonigan reached Mansfield (which it did about 4 p.m. on Sunday, the 27th October), the populace were thrown into a state of the most terrible excitement at the receipt of the almost incredible tidings, and, as may be imagined, the worst effect was produced on Mrs. Kennedy, who was reduced to a state of unspeakable wretchedness from the suspense she was left in as to the fate of her husband, who, according to McIntyre was last seen exchanging shots with the gang.

The most terrible forebodings as to the manner of his probable end were indulged in, though how and why they were encouraged or set afloat it would be impossible to say with certainty. At any rate, anticipations of his ultimate escape were scarcely entertained, which was reasonable enough, considering the number of his foes.

Mr. Sub-Inspector Pewtress, with truly admirable, and by no means common, promptitude, at once organized an armed party to search for the bodies of the slain and the missing man.

This force, which numbered 13 or 14, including three of the police, among whom was McIntyre, were very insufficiently armed, considering the persons they might have to deal with, but were unable to provide themselves with any better equipment, owing to the dearth of weapons in the township and the police camp; and it is said by some that, had the supply of arms been greater, the number of volunteers would have been augmented. So rapidly, however, were matters pushed on by Mr. Pewtress, who, for a time, seemed almost ubiquitous, that the party was enabled to start between five and six in the afternoon for the scene of the murders.

Some of the residents are reported – we do not know with what truth – to have expressed apprehensions lest, in the then defenceless state of the village, the Kellys might come down "like the wolf on the fold", and make a raid on the bank and the stores; and some of the most absurd suggestions were hazarded, such as to the likelihood of the gang burning the township and slaughtering the inhabitants, but they did not, we believe, go so far as to anticipate being scalped or eaten.

By what chain of reasoning the good folks arrived, at the possibility of the bushrangers carrying fire and sword, as it were, into an undefended and unoffending hamlet, does not appear; but had commonsense been in the ascendant, it would have shown that the looting of the bank, and perhaps a shop or two, was the worst that could be, and that remotely, on the cards.

Too much credit cannot be accorded to the local sub-inspector for the intelligence and energy he displayed in connection with the emergency, more especially seeing that, at the time of the occurrence, not only, had he recently arrived in the district from Melbourne, where his many years' residence – in fact, since his arrival in the colony – had precluded the possibility of gaining any experience in bush duty, but also that he was suffering from an indisposition of some standing. Yet he carried his operations to a successful issue, apparently by intuition in some points, save the one which has proved a stumbling block to the whole police force, from the Chief Commissioner downwards – namely, the capture of the perpetrators of the police murders. At eight o'clock on the following morning the telegraph flashed the intelligence of the unusual event through the land, and by the same means it was learned that Constable Meehan, who had been despatched on Sunday to Benalla for reinforcements by Sub-Inspector Pewtress, had not reached his destination. Before long, rumour was rife that he had fallen into the hands of the gang or some of their emissaries. He was tied up to a tree – he was shot – he was roasted – all sorts of fates were prognosticated for him, in fact, the multiplicity of the suggestions might have brought to mind the account of the various endings described in Ingoldsby's legend of "Nell Cook":

> *"Some got drowned, the some got shot, and some got broken necks –*
> *One got run over by a coach,*
> *And one, beyond the seas,*
> *Got scrapped to death with oyster shells*
> *Among the Carribees."*

But, fortunately, it turned out that the dreadful suspicions were groundless, for it was eventually learned that Meehan's non-appearance at the time he ought to have arrived was due to a – perhaps not unnatural – delusion he had suffered from.

It appears that, when about a third of the way on his road, he observed in the distance two men on horseback following him at a smart pace. Joining this to the fact that he was near the residence of a connection of the Kellys – in reality one of the most harmless and respectable men in the district – he concluded that the persons he saw were the Kellys, or some of their friends, in hot pursuit.

He immediately set spurs to his horse, when to his horror, his pursuers, as he thought, increased their pace to a gallop. Being unarmed – having lent his revolver to McIntyre – and seeing that they gained on him, he turned off the road through a slip-panel, and then, casting his horse adrift, took to his heels, and gaining the shelter of the bush, hid there till dark. He then took his boots off and travelled all night, across swamps, over rocks, through scrub, and, in fact, meeting all kinds of disagreeable impediments, as he was afraid to return to the road, and therefore continued his course across country; when, after travelling some 25 miles in this way, he reached Benalla in the course of the following day.

It came out that two ferocious highwaymen were the innocent sons of a neighbouring squatter, who, being astonished at seeing the man fly at their approach, quickened their pace in order to find out who it was, and why he bolted.

When, at last, they saw him desert his horse and betake himself to the bush, they set him down as some lunatic; so, out of kindness, they caught his horse and put it into a paddock belonging to a Mr. Hickson, close by. It was found by this gentleman, who, recognizing it as police property, brought it into Mansfield the next day. The foregoing incident had, doubtless, a ludicrous side to it, yet it cannot be denied that Meehan, as the bearer of important dispatches, adopted the proper course, although he argued from false premises.

He is said to have got awfully chaffed by his comrades at Benalla on the subject, one "merrie jester", belonging to the detective branch, telling him that he wasn't half a man that didn't hand up his coat and put a couple of bullet holes through it, in proof of his miraculous escape.

When intelligence of the murders was telegraphed to Mr. Secretan, of the detective department, he at once wired back instructions to send out police and arrest the criminals; but, owing to unforeseen circumstances, the letter portion of his order was not carried out.

Constable McIntyre

CHAPTER XV

"According to his virtue let us use him,
With all respect and rites of burial."
-Shakespeare

The search party under the command of Mr. Sub-Inspector Pewtress and guidance of Constable McIntyre, whose pluck alone must have supported his bruised and jaded frame through the expedition, reached the desired locality shortly after two o'clock on Monday morning.

Here, they had some little difficulty in finding the bodies owing to the darkness, for, in addition to lighting matches, which were almost useless on account of the wind, the searchers had to feel about the ground for the objects they sought. On finding the corpses of the two constables they enveloped them in bagging, and packed them on horseback to the Wombat saw-mills, a distance of about seven miles, through a terribly difficult country, rendered trebly so by the intense darkness.

Here they were met by Mr. Thomas McMillan, who had driven a drag, with four horses, to meet them (this being the nearest accessible point for wheeled vehicles), and by that gentleman they were conveyed to Mansfield.

A search in the neighbourhood of the scene, as accurate as the darkness would allow, failed to bring to light any traces of the missing sergeant, though from subsequent observations it was evident some of the party must have been within a short distance of his remains.

Starting at day-break from the saw-mills, some of the party reached Mansfield about noon, and were followed shortly afterwards by the rest and Mr. McMillan's drag with the dead troopers.

When the bodies, the clothing of which was caked with congealed blood, were taken to the morgue, they were visited and viewed by a vast concourse, who were loud in their denunciations of the Kelly gang.

The countenances of the dead presented a calm and peaceful appearance, as if of sleep, except that Lonigan's exhibited a slight expression of being in thought about some puzzling question, as though the subject of some dream were occupying his mind.

On the following morning Dr. Reynolds made a post mortem examination, and at the succeeding magisterial inquiry, held at the hospital by H. H. Kitchen, Esq., J.P., the inevitable conclusion was arrived at that the two constables had come to their death by gunshot wounds inflicted by the bushrangers.

Mrs. Lonigan arrived in Mansfield on Monday, in a state of grief and mental agony, which it would be difficult to describe, and the greatest sympathy was evinced for her in her sad and sudden bereavement.

Following the inquiry, the funerals of the dead constables took place at the Mansfield Cemetery, and were attended by a large number of residents and others. Lonigan, we understand, was personally known to but very few on the spot, but was spoken of by those few as an honest, plucky man, well liked in his own neighbourhood; but Scanlon, we gather, was as universally known in Mansfield (where he had been stationed for many years) as he was respected, and his untimely end was regretted sincerely by all.

Shortly after ten a.m. on the morning of the same day, a search party, numbering about twenty, headed by Mr. Sub-Inspector Pewtress, who had been scarcely out of the saddle since Sunday afternoon, proceeded to look for the missing Sergeant Kennedy; but their labour was in vain, and they returned to Mansfield shortly before midnight, having left four constables at the Wombat saw-mills, on the watch.

At four o'clock on Wednesday, another party, headed by Janes Tomkins, Esq., president of the Mansfield Shire, and Sub-Inspector Pewtress, accompanied by several residents, started in search of Kennedy, taking with them provisions for some days. On the following morning, about eight o'clock, the body of the unfortunate sergeant was found by a Mr. Henry G. Sparrow, in the place and position described in a previous chapter. The body was placed in some bagging, and packed to the saw-mills, in the same manner as the others, and brought in a spring cart to the Mansfield Morgue, where, on Friday, an inspection of the body by Dr. Reynolds showed that death was the result of a gunshot wound in the chest. The usual inquiry was held. The head and face of the corpse, which was in an advanced state of decomposition, presented a shocking appearance, being swollen and discoloured so as almost to defy recognition, while the fleshy part of the nose and the right ear had been eaten away by insects.

It is worthy of record that the Chief Commissioner of Police had offered (irrespective of the search parties) a reward of £30 for information of Kennedy, which was supplemented by private liberality, and, thereupon, a young man in the district, who was acquainted with some connections of the Kellys, undertook to gain the required tidings on condition that the money should be handed over to Mrs. Skillion, the wife of W. Skillion, who was convicted of attempting to murder Constable Fitzpatrick in October last; the unfortunate woman, whose sole support was her husband, being left in very straitened circumstances. However, as this volunteer was on his road to Greta, Kennedy's remains arrived at Mansfield.

The body of Sergeant Kennedy was interred at the Mansfield Cemetery between two and three o'clock in the afternoon, and was attended by 200 persons, more or less. The procession was headed by the Bishop of Melbourne, supported by the Rev. Father Scanlon and the Rev. Mr. Sandiford, Church of England clergyman. The Rev. Mr. Reid, Presbytarian clergyman, also joined in the procession.

The coffin was profusely decorated with floral offerings; the majority had been, with thoughtful solicitude, prepared by a young lady of the district, who was a friend of Mrs. Kennedy's; and, besides, Mrs. Moorhouse, the wife of the Bishop, provided a handsome wreath, which she sent for the same purpose to the sorrowing widow.

It would be taking an unwarrantable liberty with the privacy of the bereaved families, were we to attempt a delineation of their griefs; but we may be permitted to add to the universally-expressed satisfaction our congratulations on the fact that the Government, recognising the exceptionally heartrending character of the catastrophe, decided upon rendering such pecuniary assistance as may, in some degree, lessen the horrors involved in their loss.

The three murdered constables were in the prime of life, and of long standing in the force, of which they were considered valuable members.

The survivor, who joined the police in 1869, though possessed of less experience, perhaps, has made himself a favourite with those who know him, and probably stands proportionately high in official estimation. Kennedy leaves a wife, and five young children, Lonigan a wife and four children, while Scanlon and McIntyre were single men.

On the same day McIntyre was dispatched to the Richmond Depot Hospital, both for the purpose of recovering from his injuries and the severe shock sustained by his system, and also to guard him from any attack on his life by the outlaws or their friends, he being the only witness in connection with the murders.

Since then he has, fortunately, recovered his health and strength, and has frequently expressed a strong desire to join some one of the parties detached in pursuit of the gang.

CHAPTER XVI

"What! Frightened with false fire?"
- Shakespeare

"The Mansfield Scare!"; "The Mansfield Murders!"; "The Mansfield Tragedy!" - are the expressions which have been largely used by the public prints in connection with the murder of the police in the Wombat Ranges.

Now, with regard to the first, a great deal of twaddle and humbug has been written, and perhaps, too, in some quarters believed; but from reliable information, we feel assured that, although a feeling of horror and detestation at the massacre, and sympathy with the sufferers, pervaded the district, yet the "scare" was almost a myth. To believe, as was reported, that many of the business men kept watch over their stores by night at the time of the great excitement, would involve the absurd inference that any of them would venture, for one moment, to resist the Kellys, had they made a raid on them soon after the tragedy; while the real fact is said to be that not unfrequently might be heard some such remark as this – "What a lark if the Kellys were to stick up the bank tonight, and help themselves to tucker at some of the stores!" In fact, we have come to the conclusion that the "scare" was chiefly confined to the hysterical lady celebrated by the local organ, who, thinking she heard four men riding, shouting, through the High Street one night, cried out in accents of the wildest terror, "The Kellys (or "the Murderers" we forget which) are coming!" a phase of the "scare" which, we apprehend, a bucket of cold water judiciously applied would instantly have done away with, and which is now found to have been caused by a deaf and dum brother of a young man, called, from his eccentricities, "Wild" Wright, who was galloping home, vociferating as he went, according to his cheerful wont.

But as nothing, no matter how apparently mean or insignificant, is created without an object, so the imagination involved "scare" effected one beneficial purpose; for the ventilation and advertising of the "scare" had for their consequence an influx and residence of large bodies of police, with their horses, which exercised a most beneficial influence on local trade – already tolerably good, all things considered, yet not so extensive as to offer any objection to its augmentation.

If, however, we are misled, and the "scare" really did exist, how can we reconcile the fact with the following extract from the Mansfield Guardian and North-Eastern District Advocate, of 2nd November?

"The people of Mansfield deserve the greatest credit for the ready and prompt assistance they rendered in risking their lives to search for the bodies and track the murderers". The italics are our own.

Again, why the "murders" and the "tragedy" should receive the distinctive name of "Mansfield", is not easy of solution – we give it up; for the scene of the fearful drama to which the designation refer is not only 17 miles distant from Mansfield proper in a direct line, but it is not even within the corporate limits of the shire to which it lends its name.

Of the victims of the crime, only one was stationed at Mansfield, although the survivor was stationed at the same place. Further, it can scarcely have been deemed desirable for the local journal, at any rate, to specially invest the locality with such unenviable celebrity, seeing that the district – if its annals be written true – has, within the last 20 years, contributed its full quota of crime, of every shade and variety, to the statistics of the colony. We can only, therefore, attribute the fact to a morbid desire to attach a spurious notoriety to an otherwise comparatively untalked-about little village.

As a matter of fact, there was more "scare", and especially excitement, at Benalla, Wangaratta, Beechworth, and other places in that direction, than at Mansfield; and also in Melbourne the excitement was more sustained in its original intensity until, possibly, the services of the Volunteer Artillery were secured for protection along the North-Eastern line.

Search Party

CHAPTER XVII

"What! Is he fled? Go, some, and follow him;
And he that brings his head unto the king,
Shall have a thousand crowns for his reward"
- Shakespeare

By this time the township along the upper part of the North-Eastern line, as well as Mansfield, began to bristle with constables in plain clothes, carrying, on all occasions – indeed, for all we can tell, when in bed – one or two revolvers at their belts, a very judicious precaution, no doubt, but a proceeding, in the case of those wearing short coats, which would lead the uninitiated, after a cursory glance at that portion of the troopers' bodies described as being equally indecorous to turn on a friend or an enemy, to the conclusion that, either specimens of the missing link had been found, or that the artificial caudal embellishments affected by the swells among the Papuans had come into vogue.

It would be tedious for us to detail, and still more so for our readers to wade through, the monotonous adventures of the various parties of police despatched from different points to capture or annihilate the Kelly gang; but it is certain that they included a number of men amply sufficient to eat the fugitives when caught, without risking any stomachic disarrangement from overloading the digestive organs. Before this could be affected, however, they would have had to follow the preliminary instructions given in Mrs. Glass's Cookery Book anent the roasting of a hare – namely, "First catch your hare".

When we state that each party had a fair share of being "on the track" at one time or another, and invariably failed in being able to follow it to a satisfactory issue, we offer a pretty correct abstract of the proceedings that, up to this time, have taken place.

There was one "raid", nevertheless, that stands out distinctively from the others, the particulars of which will probably prove interesting to our readers, and will be found inimitably described in the following excerpt, which is from the pen of the Argus correspondent, and dated Benalla, 7th November:–

"The police have had information respecting the Kelly gang in their possession during the past day or two, but it was not considered desirable to make use of it, owing to its doubtful character, until yesterday, when corroborative reports were received, and it was then felt that there was every probability of securing the ruffians. Superintendents Nicolson and Sadleir having this knowledge in their possession, had arranged for a strong party to proceed to the district indicated, which, it may now be said, was about midway between Beechworth and Eldorado, on what is known as Reed's Creek. Here are living two or three families, who, if not directly connected with the Kelly gang by family ties, are known to be close friends of theirs, and the idea was to pay them a sudden domiciliary visit with the exception of finding some of the gang with them. The matter was kept very secret. Captain Standish, the Chief Commissioner of Police, arrived at Benalla by the afternoon train yesterday, to confer as to the best steps to be taken. As soon as Captain Standish arrived he was met by Mr. Nicolson, Mr. Sadleir having earlier in the day gone on to Beechworth to make the necessary arrangements, and as soon as the whole of the facts were laid before him he fully coincided with the views of his two officers, and it was arranged that the plan should be at once carried out. Unfortunately it has failed, but there can be no doubt that this is, in a great measure, due to the fact that the Kellys have their spies and sympathisers in all parts of the district, so that as soon as any information leaks out, or any movement is noticed, information is at once conveyed to them. For instance, when Captain Standish arrived by the train in the evening, two of the Lloyds were seen on the platform; and again subsequently, as will be seen later on, the same party inopportunely put in an appearance, and attempted – by cutting the railway telegraph wires – to frustrate the object of the expedition.

"About two p.m. notice was sent quickly round to all the troopers available in Benalla to report themselves, with arms and horses, at the railway station at midnight, arrangements being at the same time made with the railway department to have a special train in readiness shortly after that hour to proceed to Beechworth; but when an attempt was made to communicate with that township, it was found that the wires were cut, or at any rate thrown out of circuit, and it was also found that the line of the Melbourne side of Benalla was interrupted. However, after some delay, the special train got away about 1.30 a.m. and rapid progress was made to Beechworth, which place, after a few minutes' stoppage at Wangaratta was reached soon after three o'clock. The train consisted of two horse trucks and the guard's van. In the former were 10 horses, and in the latter was the Chief Commissioner of Police, Superintendent Nicolson, nine troopers and a black tracker. Four of these men had been out in the ranges for several days previously, under the command of Sergeant Strachan, and had only returned to Benalla, and gone to rest a few hours before they were again called upon to turn out for duty. The men were, however, on the alert, and not only ready but anxious for active duty again. It must be said that the appearance of the party in the van would not have given a stranger any idea of the usual smart appearance of the Victorian police force, for had such a crowd been met on a well-frequented thoroughfare there would have been a general desire to at once hand over any valuables that might be in the possession of the travellers without any cry of "Stand and deliver!" being made.

"It should here be said that while the party was waiting on the platform for the train to get ready, three men were seen hanging about, taking stock of them. They were at once pounced upon, and upon being interrogated made some unsatisfactory replies, and were detained for the time. Beechworth was reached just as the cold grey dawn was showing over the eastern hills, and the party being here met by Superintendent Sadleir, quietly proceeded to the police camp, where the were reinforced by another strong body of police, until at last, when a departure was made, there were over 30 well-armed and determined men, together with two Black trackers. Rapid progress was made for a few miles along the southern road, and then a divergence was made to the left entering the timber, the men at the same time dividing into three parties, so as not only to push forward more rapidly, but also to cover as much ground as possible. The ground was anything but suitable for rapid progress, as in places it was quite rotten, the horses sinking at times up to their knees, while in other places patches of slippery from the recent rains, rendered it necessary for every man to keep a tight hand on his bridle, more especially as the gun or rifle carried by each man was loaded, and in readiness for use. After a few miles of such work a halt was called, just as a clearing with a large slab hut was seen in the valley below. A short consultation was held between the officers, and then the place was surrounded by a cordon, while some half-dozen, with Superintendents Nicolson and Sadleir, went to pay a morning call at the house, where it was hoped to find the Kellys. A reserve of about a dozen men was kept in hand by Captain Standish in order to give chase should the desperadoes break through the cordon drawn around them.

"A few minutes of intense anxiety, and then the report of a gun was heard. This was quite enough. No necessity for any order to advance. Each man of the party, from the Chief Commissioner to the junior trooper, instinctively drove his spurs home, and a rush was made for the house. Logs that would have been looked at twice before leaping on another occasion were taken recklessly, rotten ground was plunged through, and a sharp turn round a paddock fence showed a nasty-looking rivulet, swollen with the late rains, and with very bad ground on the taking off side. None of these were noticed, but each man, keeping a tight grip on his weapon with one hand and on his bridle with the other, galloped forward, the only anxiety being who should be in first, so as to join in the melee. The pace was terrific while it lasted, but when all pulled up at the door of the hut, and rushed it, they found, to their disgust, that the Kellys were not there, and that the report they heard had been caused by the accidental discharge of one of the guns in the anxiety of the advance party to make sure of their expected prey, whom they supposed to be in the house. This one incident very plainly shows me that the remarks that had been made about the police not desiring to come to close quarters with the Kelly gang have been quite uncalled for. (It may be argued by some that the discharge of the gun was due to nervous apprehension.) What I think is, that the men want to be held more strongly in check, or some more valuable lives will be lost. That the men desire to meet with the Kellys and their two confederates is very plain; and when the two parties do meet, I fancy the four ruffians will never be brought in alive."

Standish

CHAPTER XVIII

―――――

"Dare you suspect me, whom the thought would kill?
Search then, the room' – Alphonso said, "I will!'
He searched, and searched, and found – no matter what,
It was not what he sought – "
– Don Juan

The Argus correspondent goes on to say:–

"The house to which such an unceremonious visit had been paid was that of a man named Skerritt, who is well known to have long been intimately connected with the Kellys, and whose eldest daughter was to be married to one of the party now wanted by the police. The house and immediate vicinity were closely searched, but with no success. Of course the man Skerritt put on a virtuously indignant air, and asked whether he ought to be suspected of harbouring such persons after having been in the police at home. As it was evident nothing was to be got at this place, a push was made for another selection some little distance off, belonging to

Skerritt, Jun., a son of the last-visited individual. Upon entering this hut, young Skerritt was not found; and from the appearance of the squalid den, the sole furniture of which consisted of a large bunk, a rough table, and stool, it was evident that neither the proprietor nor any of his acquaintances had been there that night. No time was lost in speculating upon possibilities, but the party pushed on over the ranges, and, descending a precipitous and dangerous gorge about 800 feet, came upon a green valley known as Sebastopol, having a creek running through it, and overshadowed on either side by the high ranges known as the Woolshed Ranges. A sharp turn to the left brought us in front of a slab hut situated in a nicely-cleared piece of land. This was the hut of Mrs. Byrne, who is also known to be most friendly to the Kellys, and is further said to be connected with another of the gang. She appeared at first greatly scared at seeing such a large party surround her house, but finding that she was not herself required, she became very bold and impudent. She could not, or more probably would not, give any information, and, in fact, denied all knowledge of the Kellys.

"It was now plain that information had been already forwarded to the gang that this locality was not safe for them, and that they had consequently shifted their quarters, for those who speak on authority are certain, from the information afforded them, but which unfortunately arrived too late, that the Kellys have been about this part within the last few days. That they have not crossed the Murray is quite certain; but at present there is some doubt which direction they have taken, the general opinion being that they are doubling back to their old position. Whichever way they do take, they must sooner or later show themselves, to obtain provisions, and be pounced upon. In the meantime the police officers and men are working their hardest to secure the ruffians. As nothing further could be done for the day, the whole of the men being well tired with their last few days' work, the party dispersed at Byrne's hut, Captain Standish, his officers, and some of the men returning to Beechworth, while the others separated and went to the respective points where they are stationed, and from whence they were summoned. As showing the absurd character of the statements which are made to the police officers, it may be said that

Dr. Cleary, of Beechworth, went to Superintendent Sadleir, about half-past ten o'clock last night, and reported that, while driving from Everton during the evening, seven shots were fired at him, and showed a small scratch as the effects of one of them. Of course his extraordinary story was set down to the effect of imagination, but it shows how men who are supposed to be endowed with a little common sense may be carried away by the present scare. Captain Standish returned to town by the afternoon train. The men who were out today were greatly pleased to see him with them in the field".

In offering the foregoing graphic account of the expedition to our readers, we would point out that we would not, necessarily, endorse all the opinions with which it is interspersed. One opinion we venture to give of our own, which we anticipate will not be contradicted – namely, that had the four outlaws been attacked by the thirty police and two black trackers, some of them would have probably been shot.

Joe Byrne

CHAPTER XIX

"Can it be possible that no man saw them?
It cannot be: some villains of my court
Are of consent and sufferance in this."
- Shakespeare

It would appear, from all that can be gathered on the subject, that the police either received, on most occasions, incorrect and misleading information, or that, owing to red-tapism or some other cause, too much time was permitted to elapse before acting upon the intelligence. In any case, it seems as if the same repulsion existed between the troopers and the outlaws as between the similar poles of different magnets; for when the constables were in one place, the gang were invariably in another – notably when the Euroa Bank was "stuck up", as presently to be described, on which occasion the marauders were understood to be surrounded, at the head of the King, many miles distant, and an onslaught hourly expected.

The number of Victorian police employed on an average in hunting the Kellys was, and is, about 200, and they were supplemented by a large number of the New South Wales force, who acted in concert with them in watching the border. The fact of their all being dressed in plain clothes led at one time to the ludicrous mistake of one party of police firing on another, an error which, it is most surprising, did not occur more than once.

Another circumstance of a laughable nature is related by the Mooroopna Telegraph:– "There is said to be only a thin line of demarcation between the sublime and the ridiculous, and we have exemplifications of its truthfulness in the ludicrous episodes that have cropped up over the Mansfield tragedy. Of course, we have had lately several blue-coated gentlemen passing through Mooroopna, dressed either in Government habiliments or disguised in private clothes. A good story is told of a constable in uniform, who was walking along a deserted road, when he was quietly joined by a man who appeared to be a 'tramp', and a conversation ensued about the Kelly gang, whereupon the man said emphatically, 'Don't you say anything against Kelly, or we'll make it warm for you", at the same time looking fierce and putting his hand behind his back. The pusillanimous peeler, unlike most of the members of the force, was regularly cowed, and allowed his courage, like Bob Acres, to ooze out of his fingers' ends, or perhaps thought discretion the better part of valour. At all events, when approaching a populated part of the locality, the constable summoned up courage, and, seizing a favourable opportunity, tripped up the man and collared him, but, on searching him, nothing more murderous was found than a lucifer, to the discomfiture of the constable, who wanted, so the story runs, to lay some charge, right or wrong, against the practical joker"

Yet, notwithstanding the reward for the apprehension of the bushrangers was increased to £500 per head, with an extra bonus of £500 for the capture of Ned Kelly as an extra stimulant, the gang managed to elude their pursuers, till it seemed as if it might have been suspected by those who knew no better, that the police had read and laid to heart the old fable detailing how.

"The man that once did sell the lion's skin
While the beast lived, was killed with hunting him".

Or that, were it not that, on entering the force, a man leaves all the fraility of his original nature behind, being, as it were, born again into a new state of existence, confederates or sympathizers might be found in the ranks, which, numbering about eleven hundred, might, under any other circumstances be liable to include more than one black sheep.

In all seriousness, though, we are disposed to attribute the failures in capturing the gang to a combination of adverse circumstances, such as red-tapism, the vast amount of unreliable information received, the track-less and impracticable character of the principle haunts of the marauders, the latter being under the leadership of a daring and clever chief, and their enjoying such facilities for learning the intentions and motions of the troopers – not in the last degree to any supineness, backwardness or want of intelligence on the part of either the officers or men of the police force, who number among them many of the bravest and most intelligent men in the British dominions. It is to be hoped, though, that there are not many of them actuated by the same feelings as the two constables who, according to a correspondent of the Ovens and Murray Advertiser, in the issue of the 16th November, declared in his hearing that, if they captured the Kellys, they would tie them to a tree, and cut their ears off, in spite of any remonstrances that might be uttered by their officers.

As for the matter of the outlaws being supplied with rations and ammunition, we may make up our minds that, while they can pay, they can get what they want, though probably, were their funds exhausted, the purveyors, not seeing their way to further "esteemed orders", would sell them to the authorities, if possible. Let us bear in mind that, during the Caffir war, the enemy were supplied with arms and ammunition by some of the leading English merchants and manufacturers.

CHAPTER XX

"Glendower: I can call spirits from the vasty deep.
Hotspur: Why, so can I; or so can any man:
But will they come, when you do call for them."
– Shakespeare

Previous to the "Rat's Castle" excursion, the Government had prepared, and passed quickly through all its stages, an Outlawry Bill, under
the provisions of which an outlaw might be taken dead or alive, provided
he failed to surrender to take his trial after due notice by proclamation,
and also whereby anyone aiding such outlaw or withholding information
about him from the police was rendered liable to 15 years' imprisonment.
Under this Act, the Crown Solicitor, by instruction of the Attorney-General, made an application of the 4th of November to the Chief Justice to
issue his warrant, and grant an order calling upon the gang, severally, to
surrender on or before of 12th of November, to take their trial for murder,
which application being granted, the necessary notices and proclamations

were published in the Government Gazette, and various newspapers, circulating in the metropolis and the North-Eastern district, of which the following are examples:–

To a MAN whose name is unknown, but whose person is described as follows:– Nineteen or twenty years of age, five feet eight inches high, rather stout, complexion somewhat fair, no beard of whiskers, a few straggling hairs over face, rather hooked nose, sinister expression; supposed to be identical with William King, of Greta, in the said colony.

Whereas on the fourth day of November, one thousand eight hundred and seventy-eight, a bench warrant was issued, in pursuance of The Felons Apprehension Act 1878, under my hand and seal, in order to your answering and taking your trial for that on the twenty-sixth day of October, One thousand eight hundred and seventy-eight, at Stringybark Creek, near Mansfield, in the Northern Bailiwick of the said colony, you did, in company with one Edward Kelly and one Daniel Kelly and another man whose name is unknown, feloniously and of malice aforethought kill and murder one Michael Scanlon.

And whereas, in pursuance of The Felons Apprehension Act, 1878, I did, on the fourth day of November, One thousand eight hundred and seventy-eight, order a summons to be inserted in the Government Gazette requiring you, the said man whose name is unknown, but whose person is described as aforesaid, to surrender yourself on or before the twelfth day of November, one thousand eight hundred and seventy-eight, at Mansfield, in the said colony of Victoria, to abide your trial for the before-mentioned crime of which you, the said man, whose name is unknown, but whose person is described as aforesaid, stand accused.

These are therefore to will and require you, the said man whose name is unknown, but whose person is described as afore-said to surrender yourself on or before the twelfth day of November, one thousand eight hundred and seventy-eight, at Mansfield, in the said colony of Victoria, to abide your trial for the before-mentioned crime of which you stand accused, and hereof you are not to fail at your peril.

Given under my hand and seal, at Melbourne, this fourth day of November, in the year of our Lord one thousand eight hundred and seventy-eight.

WILLIAM F. STAWELL, Chief Justice of the Supreme Court of the Colony of Victoria.

—

To a MAN whose name is unknown, but whose person is described as follows:– Twenty-one years of age, five feet nine inches high, very fair beard, long on chin, fair complexion, hair and moustache; supposed to be identical with Charles Brown, of King River, in the said colony.

Whereas on the fourth day of November, one thousand eight hundred and seventy-eight, a bench warrant was issued in pursuance of The Felons Apprehension Act 1878, under my hand and seal, in order to your answering and taking your trial for that on the twenty-sixth day of October, one thousand eight hundred and seventy-eight, at Stringy-Bark Creek, near Mansfield, in the northern Bailiwick of the said colony, you did, in company with one Edward Kelly and One Daniel Kelly and another man whose name is unknown, feloniously and of malice afore-thought kill and murder one Michael Scanlan.

And whereas, in pursuance of The Felons Apprehension Act 1878, I did, on the fourth day of November, one thousand eight hundred and seventy-eight, order a summons to be inserted in the Government Gazette, requiring you, the said man whole name is unknown, but whose person is described as aforesaid, to surrender on or before the twelfth day of November, one thousand eight hundred and seventy-eight, at Mansfield, in the said colony of Victoria, to abide your trial for the before-mentioned crime, of which you, the said man whose name is unknown, but whose person is described as aforesaid, stand accused.

These are therefore to will and require you, the said man whose name is unknown, but whose person is described as aforesaid, to surrender yourself on or before the twelfth day of November, one thousand eight hundred and seventy-eight, at Mansfield, in the said colony of Victoria, to abide your trial for the before-mentioned crime of which you so stand accused, and hereof you are not fail at your peril.

Given under my hand and seal, at Melbourne this fourth day of November, in the year of our Lord one thousand eight hundred and seventy-eight.

WILLIAM F. STAWELL, Chief Justice of the Supreme Court of the Colony of Victoria.

—

Accordingly, the Courthouse was kept open all day on Tuesday, the 12th of November, so as to afford every facility to the outlaws for surrendering; but, with the exception of the police magistrate, the clerk of courts, the local sub-inspector, and a constable, there was scarcely any one in attendance; in fact, the crowd was as limited almost, as though the advent of the outlaws were actually anticipated.

As might have been supposed, the expectations of the townsmen were fully realised in the non-appearance of the Kellys or their mates, who are now known not to have been, to say the least, within hearing of any ordinary call inviting them to come into court. Yet they were nearer than many people imagined at the time, for although, shortly after the Wombat outrage, they made two desperate attempts to cross the Murray River – a feat they have since accomplished with profit and notoriety to themselves – still, being on both the first occasions unsuccessful, they soon sought their old refuge in the mountains between the King River and Holland's Creek. In the meantime the following proclamations were published:–

V.R.

Persons Adjudged Outlaws under the Provision of "The
Felons Apprehension Act 1878".

—

PROCLAMATION

By His Excellency SIR GEORGE FERGUSON BOWES, Knight Grand Cross of the Most Distinguished Order of Saint Michael and Saint George, Governor and Commander-in-Chief in and over the Colony of Victoria, and its Dependencies, and Vice-Admiral of the same, &c.&c.&c.&c.

Whereas under and by virtue of the provisions of The Felons Apprehension Act 1878, numbered 612, the Governor, with the advice of the Executive Council, is empowered to proclaim the fact that any person has been adjudged and declared to be an outlaw: Now, therefore I, the Governor of Victoria, with the advice of the Executive Council, do hereby proclaim that by a declaration under the hand of His Honour Sir William Foster Stawell, Chief Justice of the Supreme Court of Victoria, dated the fifteenth day of November, 1878, and filed of record in the said Supreme Court, Daniel Kelly, of Greta, in the said colony, was adjudged and declared to be an outlaw within the meaning and under the provisions of the said Act.

Given under my hand and the Seal of the Colony, this fifteenth day of November, one thousand eight hundred and seventy-eight, at Melbourne, Victoria, in the forty-second year of Her Majesty's reign.

(L.S.)

G. F. BOWEN

By His Excellency's Command.
BRYAN O'LOGHLEN,
Attorney-General
GOD SAVE THE QUEEN!

—

PROCLAMATION

By His Excellency SIR GEORGE FERGUSON, Knight Grand Cross of the Most Distinguished Order of Saint Michael and Saint George, Governor and Commander-in Chief in and over the Colony of Victoria and its Dependencies, and Vice-Admiral of the same, &c. &c. &c. &c.

Whereas under and by virtue of the provisions of The Felons Apprehension Act 1878, numbered 612, the Governor, with the advice of the Executive Council, is empowered to proclaim the fact that any person has been adjudged and declared to be an outlaw: Now, therefore, I, the Governor of Victoria, with the advice of the Executive Council, do hereby proclaim that by a declaration under the hand of His Honour Sir William Foster Stawell, Chief Justice of the Supreme Court of Victoria, dated the fifteenth day of November 1878, and filed of record in the said Supreme

Court, Edward Kelly, of Greta, in the said colony, was adjudged and declared to be an outlaw within the meaning and under the provisions of the said Act.

Given under my name and the Seal of the Colony, this fifteenth day of November, one thousand eight hundred and seventy-eight, at Melbourne, Victoria, in the forty-second year of Her Majesty's reign.

(L. S.)   G. F. BOWEN

By His Excellency's Command,
BRYAN O'LOGHLEN,
Attorney–General.
GOD SAVE THE QUEEN!

—

PROCLAMATION

By His Excellency Sir GEORGE FERGUSON BOWEN, Knight Grand Cross of the Most Distinguished Order of Saint Michael and Saint George, Governor and Commander-in-Chief in and over the Colony of Victoria and its Dependencies, and Vice-Admiral of the same, &c. &c. &c. &c.

Whereas under and by virtue of the provisions of The Felons Apprehension Act 1878, numbered 612, the Governor, with the advice of the Executive Council, is empowered to proclaim the fact that any person has been adjudged and declared to be an outlaw: Now, therefore, I, the Governor of Victoria, with the advice of the Executive Council, do hereby proclaim that by a declaration under the hand of His Honour Sir William Foster Stawell, Chief Justice of the Supreme Court of Victoria, dated the fifteenth day of November, 1878, and filed of record in the said Supreme Court, a certain man whose name is unknown, but whose person is described as follows, namely, twenty-one years of age, five feet nine inches high, very fair beard, long on chin, fair complexion, hair and moustache, supposed to be identical with Charles Brown, of King River, in the colony of Victoria, was adjudged and declared to be an outlaw within the meaning and under the provisions of the same Act.

Given under my hand and the Seal of the Colony, this fifteenth day of November one thousand eight hundred and seventy-eight, at Melbourne, Victoria, in the forty-second year of Her Majesty's reign.

(L.S.)   G. F. Bowen

By His Excellency's Command.
BRYAN O'LOGHLEN,
Attorney-General.
GOD SAVE THE QUEEN!

—

PROCLAMATION

By His Excellency SIR GEORGE FERGUSON BOWEN, Knight Grand Cross of the Most Distinguished Order of Saint Michael and Saint George, Governor and Commander-in-Chief in and over the Colony of Victoria and its Dependencies, and Vice-Admiral of the same, &c. &c. &c. &c.

Whereas under and by virtue of the provisions of The Felons Apprehension Act 1878, numbered 612, the Governor, with the advice of the Executive Council, is empowered to proclaim the fact that any person has been adjudged and declared to be an outlaw: Now, therefore, I the Governor of Victoria, with the advice of the Executive Council, do hereby proclaim that by a declaration under the hand of His Honour Sir William Foster Stawell, Chief Justice of the Supreme Court of Victoria, dated the fifteenth day of November, 1878, and filed of record in the said Supreme Court, a certain man whose name is unknown, but whose person is described as follows, namely, nineteen or twenty years of age, five feet eight inches high, rather stout, complexion somewhat fair, no beard or whiskers, a few straggling hairs over face, rather hooked nose, sinister expression, supposed to be identical with William King, of Greta, in the colony of Victoria, was adjudged and declared to be an outlaw within the meaning and under the provisions of the said Act.

Given under my hand and the Seal of the Colony, this fifteenth day of November One thousand eight hundred and seventy-eight, at Melbourne, Victoria, in the forty-second year of Her Majesty's reign.

(L. S.)   G. F. BOWEN

By His Excellency's Command
BRYAN O'LOGHLEN.
Attorney-General
GOD SAVE THE QUEEN!

—

The Felons Apprehension Act 1878

The particular attention of all persons of the colony is directed to the Proclamations bearing even date herewith and to above-mentioned Act, and especially to the penalties to which Daniel Kelly, Edward Kelly and the two men whose names are unknown, but who are supposed to be identical with William King, of Greta, and Charles Brown, of King River, and all persons harbouring or assisting them, or any of them, are liable under the provisions of such Act, which are as follows:–

Section 3.

If after proclamation by the Governor with the advice of the Executive Council of the fact of such adjudication shall have been published in the Government Gazette and in one or more Melbourne and one or more country newspapers such out-law shall afterwards be found at large armed or there being reasonable ground to believe that he is armed it shall be lawful for any of Her Majesty's subjects whether a constable or not and without being accountable for the using of any deadly weapon in aid of such apprehension whether its use be preceded by a demand of surrender or not to apprehend or take such outlaw alive or dead.

Section 5.

If after such proclamation any person shall voluntarily and knowingly harbour conceal or receive or give any aid shelter or sustenance to such outlaw or provide him with firearms or any other weapon or with ammunition or any horse equipment or other assistance or directly or indirectly give or cause to be given to him or any of his accomplices information tending or with intent to facilitate the commission by him of further crime or to enable him to escape from justice or shall withhold information or give false information concerning such outlaw from or to any officer of police or constable in quest of such outlaw the person so offering shall be guilty of felony and being thereof convicted shall be liable to imprisonment with or without hard labour for such period not exceeding fifteen years as the Court shall determine and no allegation or proof by the party so offending that he was at the time under compulsion

Shall be deemed a defence unless he shall as soon as possible afterwards have gone before a justice of the peace or some officer of the police force and then to the best of his ability, given full information respecting such outlaw and made a declaration on oath voluntarily and fully of the facts connected with such compulsion.

Section 7.

Any justice of the peace or officer of the police force having reasonable cause to suspect that an outlaw or accused person summoned under the provisions of this Act is concealed or harboured in or on any dwelling-house or premises may alone or accompanied by any persons acting in his aid and either by day or by night demand admission into and if refused admission may break and enter such dwelling-house or premises and therein apprehend every person whom we shall have reasonable ground for believing to be such outlaw or accused person and may thereupon seize all arms found in or on such house or premises and also apprehend all persons found in or about the same whom such justice or officer shall have reasonable ground for believing to have concealed harboured or otherwise succoured or assisted such outlaw or accused person. And all persons and arms so apprehended and seized shall be forthwith taken before some convenient justice of the peace to be further dealt with and disposed of according to law.

BRYAN O'LOGHLEN,
Attorney-General.
CROWN LAW OFICES,
Melbourne, 15th November, 1878.
TO DANIEL KELLY, of Greta, in the colony of Victoria.

Whereas, on the fourth of November, One thousand eight hundred and seventy-eight, a Bench Warrant was issued in pursuance of The Felons Apprehension Act 1878, under my hand and seal, in order to your answering and taking your trial for that, on the twenty-sixth day of October, One thousand eight hundred and seventy-eight, at Stringy-Bark Creek, near Mansfield, in the Northern Bailiwick of the said colony, you did, in company with one Edward Kelly and two other men whose names are unknown, feloniously and of malice aforethought kill and murder one Michael Scanlan.

And whereas, in pursuance of The Felons Apprehension Act 1878, I did, on the fourth day of November, one thousand eight hundred and seventy-eight, order a summons to be inserted in the Government Gazette requiring you, the said Daniel Kelly, to surrender yourself on or before the twelfth day of November, One thousand eight hundred and seventy-eight at Mansfield, in the said colony of Victoria, to abide your trial for the before-mentioned crime of which you, the said Daniel Kelly, stand accused.

These are therefore to will and require you, the said Daniel Kelly, to surrender yourself on or before the twelfth of November, One thousand eight hundred and seventy-eight, at Mansfield, in the said colony of Victoria, to abide your trial for the before-mentioned crime of which you so stand accused, and hereof you are not to fail at your peril.

Given under my hand and seal, at Melbourne, this fourth day of November, in the year of our Lord one thousand eight hundred and seventy-eight.

WILLIAM F. STAWELL, Chief Justice of the Supreme Court of the Colony of Victoria.

—

To EDWARD KELLY, of Greta, in the colony of Victoria.

Whereas on the fourth day of November, one thousand eight hundred and seventy-eight, a Bench Warrant was issued in pursuance of The Felons Apprehension Act 1878, under my hand and seal, in order to your answering and taking your trial for that on the twenty-sixth day of October, One thousand eight hundred and seventy-eight, at Stringy-Bark Creek, near Mansfield, in the Northern Bailiwick of the said colony, you did, in company with one Daniel Kelly and two other men whose names are unknown, feloniously and of malice afore-thought kill and murder one Michael Scanlan.

And whereas, in pursuance of The Felons Apprehension Act 1878, I did, on the fourth day of November, one thousand eight hundred and seventy-eight, order a summons to be inserted in the Government Gazette, requiring you, the said Edward Kelly, to surrender yourself on or before the twelfth day of November, one thousand eight hundred and seventy-eight, at Mansfield, in the said colony of Victoria, to abide your trial for the before-mentioned crime, of which you, the said Edward Kelly, stand accused.

These are therefore to will and require you, the said Edward Kelly, to surrender yourself on or before the twelfth day of November, one thousand eight hundred and seventy-eight, at Mansfield, in the said colony of Victoria, to abide your trial for the before-mentioned crime, of which so you stand accused, and hereof you are not to fail at your peril.

Given under my hand and seal, at Melbourne, this fourth day of November, in the year of our Lord one thousand eight hundred and seventy eight.

WILLIAM F. STAWELL, Chief Justice of the Supreme Court of the Colony of Victoria.

—

The following account, which we borrow from the Ovens and Murray Advertiser of the 16th November, gives a very excellent epitome of their movements about the time:—

"After remaining for a time in their old haunts, they appear to have made up their minds to make a dash Murraywards, and endeavour to cross into the sister colony; but in this attempt, they were frustrated, partly through the floods, and partly through the fact that nearly all the passable crossing places were closely watched. It is know that they remained from Wednesday, the 6th, to Friday the 9th, in the neighbourhood of Barnawartha, and there is undoubtedly some truth in the story told by Margery.

"Margery is a selector near the Murray. On his way backwards and forwards to the river last Tuesday, he saw four men near a lagoon. He had some talk with them. They said at first they were police, and afterwards one of them stated that he was Kelly. They showed handcuffs, and he saw that they carried fire-arms in their swags, as many shearers do. He had a long talk with them, and they got some loaves of bread and a bottle of wine from him, but made no demand for provisions, and did not stick him up. He told them that if they were the Kellys they had better clear out, as that was no place for them. They stayed some time at the lagoon, and kept him there also. Before he went up to them, he had seen them on his way to the river, where he had set some fishing lines, and he passed once or twice before he had the curiosity to see who they were.

"Finding it impossible to get across the river, and deeming it safer to get back to their old well-known haunts, they then retraced their steps, and stayed for a few hours only in the locality of Sheep Station Creek, not far from Beechworth, but were moving long before the ill-planned and clumsily-carried-out raid, when the police army stormed the habitations of the Skerritts and the Byrnes. Thence, fully seised with the police movements, they journeyed back again and actually passed through Wangaratta, at the time when the greater number of the police were away. They stayed for a time on the One-Mile Creek, and then made their way to Warby's Ranges, where they cast adrift one of the troop horses, which was afterwards found by the police under Inspector Smith". From this place they crossed the railway near Glenrowan, and made their way to the neighbourhood of their original haunts in the Wombat Ranges.

CHAPTER XXI

"Let not a monument give you or me hopes,
Since not a pinch of dust remains of Cheops"
- Don Juan

Some time after the three police had met their death, several of the Mansfield residents came to the conclusion that the circumstances of the case demanded the erection of a monument to the memory of the dead, the result of which was a meeting of the subject and the subsequent publication of the accompanying advertisement:–

THE MANSFIELD POLICE MURDERS

—

MURDERED POLICE MEMORIAL FUND

—

IN MEMORY OF THE THREE BRAVE FELLOWS WHO LOST THEIR LIVES IN THE EXECUTION OF THEIR DUTY IN THE WOMBAT RANGES, ON OCTOBER 26th, 1878

—

Memorial Fund Committee:

HENRY H. KITCHEN, J.P., Mansfield, Chairman.

JAMES H. GRAVES, M.P. for Delatite.

JAMES TONKINS, Junior, J.P., President Mansfield Shire Council.

JAMES SHAW, J.P., Mansfield.

HENRY PEWTRESS, Sub-Inspector of Police, Mansfield.

GEORGE W. HALL, Proprietor Mansfield Guardian.

TREASURER – M. L. ASHE, Manager Bank of New South Wales.

SECRETARY – J. H. A. HAGEMAN, Secretary Mansfield Shire Council.

BANKERS – Bank of New South Wales, Mansfield.

—

In Memory of the Three Brave Fellows – Sergeant MICHAEL KENNEDY, and Constables MICHAEL SCANLAN and THOMAS LONIGAN – who were so brutally murdered by the Kelly gang, while in the execution of their duty in the Wombat Ranges, near Mansfield, on the 26th October last, it has been thought meet to erect a monument in a suitable locality at Mansfield, and the above-named gentlemen have consented to act as a committee to carry out all matters in connection with the movement, and to raise funds by voluntary contributions for that purpose.

The merit of the case of the present appeal to the public is doubtlessly sufficiently known and acknowledged to ensure ready and general support, but special attention is directed to the following particulars:–

1st. No contributions are herein asked for in aid of the bereaved families of the unfortunate men, as the Government has already promised adequately to provide for them.

2nd. That the deceased men died in the execution of their duty, and died bravely.

3rd. That the duty in the execution whereof Sergeant KENNEDY and Constables SCANLAN and LONIGAN lost their lives, was not of their seeking, but that they were specially directed by their superiors to undertake it.

4th. That they were all men of merit in the force, and chosen for the duty on that account.

5th. That this is no ordinary occasion, and requires that Public Sympathy should be shown in some substantial form to stimulate other members of the police force, and of other branches of the public service, in the performance of onerous and dangerous duties, by the knowledge that their efforts in the public service will not be unfeelingly
ignored.

The committee, therefore, with the foregoing object in view, and as the occasion is deemed to be of a national character, appeal to the people of Victoria for their practical sympathy and assistance.

Subscription lists have been generally circulated throughout the colony, and besides the collectors who hold lists, contributions will be received at the office of this Journal, by the Editor of the Melbourne Argus, the Editor of the Melbourne Age, the Editor of the Melbourne Daily Telegraph, and the Treasurer of the Memorial Fund at Mansfield.

It is intended to close the lists on the 31st January next, and all contributions contributed or obtained are respectfully requested to be sent to the Treasurer of the Fund at Mansfield by that date.

All contributions will be acknowledged by the press.

J. H. A. HAGEMAN,
Secretary.

Mansfield, 16th December, 1878.

At the same time, collection sheets were freely distributed in the chief places of business through the colony, including the banks, as well as local government corporations, private individuals, &c.

At the outset, the promoters had in view the erection of a monument pure and simple, in the township, with a suitable inscription, but soon some of the utilitarian members began to moot the desirability of making the memorial take the shape of a fountain, where, by bring a supply of pure water from the nearest available source, a lasting benefit might be bestowed on the inhabitants of Mansfield, who, barring those who have been able to afford a ground tank for rain water, are dependent for their supply on a creek which, in summer, is little more than a chain of water-holes, saturated with alkaline salts of an aperient tendency, and impreg-nated with the filth of horses, cattle, and pigs, sometimes with other and worse abominations, while in winter it is a rushing torrent of pea-soupy, chocolate-coloured mud; indeed, there is no doubt that, were it not for the liberality of the owners of artificial reservoirs, in the matter of drinking water, Mansfield would not enjoy its comparative immunity from diseases of the typhoid type.

It was anticipated, at the outset, that £1,000 would be readily col-lected; but as, at the closing of the lists, only £468.9.0 had been sent in, it may prove needful to forego the water-supply idea, unless it were possible for the Mansfield Shire Council to obtain a subsidy from the central Gov-ernment, although possibly all the lists were not in.

The scheme, originating no doubt altogether in genuine sentiments of sympathy and regret, is an admirable exponent of the feelings of the public in connection with the Wombat disasters.

In the matter of the proposed monument, Victoria has proved herself superior to New South Wales, to judge by what took place in connection with a similar, but more barbarous and extensive murder in the latter colony, leaving the shooting of Sergeant Wallings out of the question. We allude now to the case of the Clark brothers, who, however, paid the penalty of their crime on the scaffold many years ago. The particulars of the affair may be in the memory of some of our readers, but for the benefit of others we give a brief outline of it.

The Clark brothers, then, having broken out of jail at Maitland, we believe, a warder, who was regarded as a sharp man, and three constables, were sent to arrest them, and were, to that end put on their track. In the false character of surveyors they established a camp near the old haunts of the runaways. Here they remained on the look-out for some days, until a female friend of the Clarks, to whom one of the constables had paid some delicate attentions, getting an inkling of the true characters of the soi-disant surveyors, informed her friends. The next morning, before sunrise, the four men were shot dead (by the Clarks) as they lay asleep, and were subsequently buried on the banks of the adjacent creek, each rolled in a sheet of bark, it is said. The inhabitants of the neighbouring township, however, had them exhumed, and buried in consecrated ground.

The affair created a great sensation for a time, but soon became forgotten, or, at best, but rarely thought of or referred to.

CHAPTER XXII

"A famour man was Robin Hood,
The English ballad singer's joy."
- Old Song

The widely-extended and generally-expressed horror and detestation of the police murders which have been displayed through this colony, render more prominent the sympathy and admiration for the Kellys that, by the larrikin class, are not only barely disguised in some cases, but openly vaunted in others.

This is more noticeable among the youth in various large centres of population where, not content with openly avowing their feelings in simple conversation, they congregate occasionally at street corners and elsewhere to sing ballads – hymns of triumph, as it were – in their praise. We have not been informed, whether these lyrics have yet taken shape in print, but we have succeeded in obtaining the words of a few by taking them down from dictation.

They are, for the most part, wretched doggerel, void of point as a rule, and in the metre – if metre it can be called – adapted to the Universal Irish street-ballad tune, if we except one, which is an attempted parody on the "The Bould Sojer Boy". It seems to us that the majority of them are from the same pen, and we should imagine that the writer would find himself more at home in a "thieves' kitchen", a St. Giles' ballad-mongery, or one of Her Majesty's jails, than at either missionery meeting or the gathering together of a Young Men's Christian Association, unless, indeed, he attended with the intention of picking the pockets of the audience.

We venture to submit some extracts from this kind of literature merely as samples of the pernicious stuff that is provided to poison the ear.

It is not so much any distortion of facts that will be found to excite disgust, but rather the flippant phraseology in which the descriptions of events of serious import are clothed.

We have limited our extracts to the most harmless portions to be selected from the mass of leprous distilments of the composer's perverted genius, such as it is, feeling confident that the majority of readers will join in our estimate of the wretched and mischievous productions, inductively judging what the character must be of the lines we have withheld from publication, as being outside the limits of decency and order. The following lines form a portion of a bad parody on "The Bould Sojer Boy"; this sample will be enough of the song to judge by. It refers, of course, to the Kelly gang:–

> *Oh, there's not a dodge worth knowing,*
> *Or showing, that's going,*
> *But You'll learn (this isn't blowing)*
> *From the bold K—y G—g.*
> *We have mates where 'er we go*
> *That, somehow, let us know*
> *The approach of every foe*
> *To the bold K—y G—g.*
> *There's not a peeler riding*
> *Wombat ranges, hill or siding,*
> *But would rather far be hiding,*

Though he'd like to see us hang.
We thin their ranks,
We rob the banks,
And say no thanks,
For what we do.
Oh, the terror of the camp is the bold K—y G—g.
Then, if you want a spree,
Come with me, and you'll see
How grand it is to be
In the bold K—y G—g.

The next is a fragment of an account of the Euroa bank robbery, and possesses the negative advantage of containing less pernicious stuff than most of the other effusions:–

So Kelly marched into the bank,
A cheque all in his hand,
For to have it changed for money
Of Scott he did demand.
And when that he refused him,
He, looking at him straight,
Said, "See here, my name's Ned Kelly,
And this here man's my mate".
With pistols pointed at his nut,
Poor Scott did stand amazed,
His stick he would have liked to cut,
But was with funk half crazed;
The poor cashier, with real fear,
Stood, trembling at the knees,
But at last they both seen 'twas no use,
And handed out the keys.
The safe was quickly gutted then,
The drawers turned out, as well,
The Kellys being quite polite,
Like any noble swell.
With flimsies, gold and silver coin,

> *The threepennies, and all,*
> *Amounting to two thousand pounds,*
> *They made a glorious haul.*

A portion of a ballad, professedly descriptive of what occurred in the Wombat Ranges, and a verse from "The Wild Colonial Boy", will bring these examples to an end:—

> *A sergeant and three constables set out from Mansfield town,*
> *Near the end of last October, for to hunt the Kellys down;*
> *So they travelled to the Wombat, and they thought it quite a lark,*
> *And they camped upon the borders of a creek called "Stringy Bark".*
> *They had grub and ammunition there to last them many a week,*
> *And next morning two of them rode out, all to explore the creek;*
> *Leaving M'Intyre behind them, at the camp, to cook the grub,*
> *And Lonigan to sweep the floor, and boss the washing-tub.*
> *It was shortly after breakfast Mac thought he heard the noise,*
> *So gun in hand, he sallied out, to try and find the cause;*
> *But he never saw the Kellys planted safe behind a log,*
> *So he slithered back to smoke and yarn, and wire into prog.*
> *But bold Kelly and his comrades thought they'd like a nearer look,*
> *For, being short of grub, they wished to interview the cook;*
> *And of fire-arms and cartridges they found they had too few,*
> *So they longed to grab the pistols, guns, and ammunition too.*
> *Both the bobbies, at a stump alone, they then were pleased to see,*
> *A-watching of the billy boiling for the troopers' tea;*
> *There they smoked and chatted gaily, never thinking of alarms,*
> *Till they heard the fearful cry behind, "Bail up! Throw up your arms!"*
> *The traps they started wildly, and Mac then firmly stood,*
> *And threw up his arms, while Lonigan made tracks to gain the wood;*
> *Reaching round for his revolver, but before he touched the stock,*
> *Ned Kelly drew his trigger, shot, and dropped him like a cock.*
> *Then, after searching M'Intyre, all through the camp they went,*
> *And cleared the guns and cartridges and pistols from the tent;*
> *But brave Kelly muttered sadly, as he loaded up his gun,*
> *"Oh, what a —— pity that the —— tried to run!"*

One verse of "The Wild Colonial Boy" will give a sufficient idea of the style of the whole song.

> *He took a pistol from his belt,*
> *And waved that lovely toy;*
> *"I'll shoot, but not surrender!"*
> *Says the bold colonial boy.*

"Let who will make their laws, so long as I make their ballads", was a remark made by one who knew human nature; and we may be sure that such pestiferous stuff as we have given expurgated extracts from exercises an influence upon our youth which statutory enactments fail, by a long way, in being able to counteract.

Steve Hart, Dan Kelly, Ned Kelly

CHAPTER XXIII

"P. Henry – Your money.
Poins   – Villains!
P. Henry – Got with much ease. Now merrily to horse"
- Shakespeare

Although the Kelly party returned to their original haunts after their fruitless attempts to cross the Murray, they did not rest there for any length of time, but betook themselves to the Strathbogie Ranges and the hilly country extending southward thence towards the Goulburn, included by the Puzzle Ranges, and the vicinity of Miller's Ponds and Cathkin Stations. Here they remained securely for some three weeks in various hiding places, during a great part of which time their chief commissary was a Chinaman whom, although they had pressed into the service, they also liberally rewarded both, for his risk and labour. It was during this period the plan of sticking up of the National Bank of Euroa, having for its preliminary the taking possession of Faithful Creek Station, as a basis of operations, was brought to maturity. The station in question is the property of Mr. Younghusband.

On the night of Sunday, the 7th of December, the guard camped not very many miles from Euroa, in the ranges, and from thence made a descent on the station, which is about three miles to the north-east of the township, and close to the railway line.

About 12.30 pm. on the following Monday, a man walked to the homestead at the station, and asked the first man whom he encountered (one of the station hands) whether the overseer, Mr. Macauley, was about. Receiving a reply in the negative, he walked away a short distance, and returned again. The man whom he questioned then informed him that Mr. Macauley was expected home in the evening, and that if it was anything particular the stranger wanted, he himself might be able to assist him. To this the fellow said, "No, it is no matter". He then walked away again, and the station hand referred to (a man named Fitzgerald) was somewhat astonished, to see him beckoning to three persons, who appeared to be his mates. Two of the latter approached, leading four horses, and commenced to look suspiciously about them. Shortly afterwards, the firstcomer entered the house, and encountered a woman named Mrs. Fitzgerald, the wife of the man already referred to, who is also engaged at the station. He inquired of her how many men were about the place, and advised her at the same time to tell the truth. Upon receiving an answer, he said, "Look here, you'll have to bail up. I'm Ned Kelly, but don't be afraid, as we won't hurt you: we only want some refreshment, and feed for our horses". The poor woman was of course naturally very much alarmed, but she called her husband in, and told him what Kelly had said. Fitzgerald was completely unarmed, and Kelly, to add force to the woman's words, exhibited his revolver to the astonished labourer. Being entirely at the ruffian's mercy, Fitzgerald said that of course he was both welcome to refreshments for himself and food for his horses. Kelly then directed the man to go into a slab cottage attached to the place, and put a sentry over him. By this time another young fellow, working about the homestead, had been similarly dealt with, and shortly afterwards four other men, approaching at intervals one by one to the cottage, were incarcerated with the rest.

In the middle of the day a hawker, named James Gloster, drove up to the station, and unharnessing his horse, according to his custom on previous occasions, went into the kitchen to boil his billy. Here he found Stephen Hart sitting, of whom he had no suspicion, and after slinging the billy and having a short chat, he commenced whistling and dancing in front of the hearth, Hart occasionally inviting him to "go it" and give him another step. When the water had boiled, Gloster took the vessel, and was proceeding to his cart to get the tea, when Hart ordered him to come back, but he refused, saying, "isn't it my own billy?" However, he was quickly convinced that obedience was necessary, for on going outside he met Ned Kelly, who, after introducing himself, obliged the hawker, as well as his boy, to join the company already in custody. About this time they were startled by seeing what they supposed to be a special train stopping opposite the homestead, from which they feared they would see a party of police emerge to attack them; but only one passenger got out, and the train went on. The man turned up to be a telegraph line repairer, who had been despatched to mend the wires, which they had taken the precaution to cut, for fear of accidents. Him they quickly added to the assemblage in the slab lock-up. Some other men who time to time approached met with the same fate. Coming to the conclusion that a new rig-out was desirable, they asked Gloster to come down to his cart, and display for their approval his supply of slops, when, each man having suited himself as well as the stock would admit, they made a bonfire of their old clothes, quite as well satisfied as if the itinerant merchant had sworn, on the occasion of each article being tried on, "By —— it looks as if it was made for you, and I'm letting you have it for less than it cost me", the latter part of which would have been strictly true. The overseer came riding home at half-past four o'clock, and, whilst crossing a bridge leading to the cottages was struck with the somewhat quiet appearance of the place. Being, however, under no apprehension of danger, he took no notice, and reined up almost opposite one of the doors. Fitzgerald then put his head out, and told him the Kellys were there, and Ned Kelly came out at once and confronted the overseer. Some conversation took place between the bushranger and Macauley, during which the latter stated that he did not believe he was

Ned Kelly. Upon looking at the other members of the gang, he, however, at once recognized Daniel Kelly. Macauley was then in like manner as the others taken prisoner, but was not shut up with the rest, one of the desperadoes keeping an especial eye upon him. The Kellys informed him that they did not want to shoot anybody, unless they were forced to do so, and only wanted to use the station as a camping ground for the purpose of resting themselves and their horses. The animals which they rode were very valuable ones, as the overseer remarked to them, and said that they did not look as if they wanted much feeding. "Oh, yes; we can always get good horses when we want them", was the candid reply.

In the evening the bushrangers made themselves quite at home, but still kept a sharp look-out against any surprise. They had supper, as had also their prisoners, the whole party appearing jolly and unconcerned, Edward Kelly talking nearly all the night through; and although his mates took a sleep in turns he was never observed to lie down at all. In the morning the gang appeared to be in high spirit: and busied themselves in cleaning their guns and revolvers. They were all armed to the teeth, and Ned Kelly carried the late Sergeant Kennedy's repeating rifle.

After sticking up the Faithful Creek Station, it appears that the Kelly gang gathered about twenty-two persons altogether to prevent the alarm being spread, and after placing one of the gang (a ruffian named Byrne) in charge, with loaded fire-arms in his possession, the other three men – namely Edward and Daniel Kelly, and Steven Hart – started for the bank at Euroa with the hawker's cart on Tuesday morning.

At the slip panels giving egress from the station, they met two farmers in a spring cart, whom they stopped and ordered to get down, emphasizing the command with the information from their leader that he was Ned Kelly. One of the farmers, disbelieving their statements, was profane enough to explain, "That be d——d!" Whereupon Kelly produced a convincing argument, carrying much weight, in the shape of six ball cartridges, which thoroughly purged the sceptic of any doubts on the matter; and the passengers were at once escorted to durancevile, after which the three bushrangers, having annexed the conveyance and horses, proceeded on their expedition.

The hawker's boy was taken with them in his father's cart, which was driven by Daniel Kelly, while the elder Kelly drove the spring cart, accompanied by Hart on horseback. Hart entered Euroa first, and, after having his dinner at the North-Eastern Hotel without, apparently, being known, he joined the brothers Kelly in the afternoon, and the three went at once to the bank. Ned Kelly drove to the front door of the bank, Dan Kelly drove into the back yard, while Hart rode to the front of the public house, and fastened his horse there. Mr. Scott and his family were about to leave the house for a short time, when Edward Kelly knocked at the front door of the bank (which adjoins Mr. Scott's private residence) and the door was shortly afterwards opened by Mr. Bradley, the accountant. Ned Kelly presented a cheque, bearing the signature of Mr. Macauley, the overseer of the Faithful Creek Station. Mr. Bradley told him that it was after banking hours (being then past four o'clock) and Kelly then asked to see Mr. Scott. Mr. Bradley showed Kelly into the office, where Mr. Scott was engaged writing, and Kelly then announced who he was, and ordered Mr. Scott to "bail up" and throw his hands up. The same intimation was given to Mr. Bradley and the clerk. Kelly had just before been joined by Hart, who entered by the back door, and they both covered Mr. Scott and the others by presenting loaded revolvers, with a threat to shoot them if they attempted any resistance. Mr. Bradley was also ordered to give up all the money they had; but, after consulting Mr. Scott, Kelly was told that nothing would be given them, although they could not perhaps be prevented from taking all they could get hold of. Kelly at once instituted a search, and succeeded in getting £300 in notes, gold and silver, after which he intimated his intention of searching the rest of the premises. Mr. Scott threatened to strike Kelly if he did so, as it might give a great fright to the ladies, and Mr. Scott was then allowed to go to the door of the room where the family were, and cautioned them not to be alarmed, at the same time telling them who the visitors were. The ladies took Mr. Scott's advice, and did not betray any serious alarm, although they felt anything but comfortable.

Kelly and Hart having had some spirits and water, then separated, Ned Kelly going into the private residence, while Hart remained guard over the prisoners in the office, while Dan Kelly stood near the door. Ned Kelly, after being refused any more money, said that he felt sure there was more to be got, and, having obtained the keys of the strong room, he succeeded in getting 31 ozs. of gold, besides the following reserve cash:– £680 in £10 notes, £335 in £5 notes, £418 in £1 notes, £311 in gold, and £9.8.6 in silver; total £1,943. 8. 6d. The numbers of the notes are not known. The hawker's boy continued running backward and forward during all these proceedings, and seemed to take a tolerably active interest in what was going on. Kelly bundled the whole of the booty into a sack, but he did not touch any of the bills or securities that were in the bank. Mr. Scott was then called upon to bring out his horse, and harness it to his private buggy, but he declined, and Kelly said he would do it himself. He did so, and after a short delay, a start was made with the two clerks, a female servant and Dan Kelly, in the hawker's cart; Mrs. Scott and seven children, and Mrs. Scott''s mother, in the buggy; and Mr. Scott, Ned Kelly and a female servant (by whom Hart was recognized), in the spring cart, where the sack of money was, and Hart on horse-back in the rear. Before leaving the bank Mr. Scott endeavoured to delay the departure by inducing the Kellys to have something to drink, but in this he was only partially successful. Ned Kelly accepted a glass of whisky, but before drinking it he insisted upon Mr. Scott taking some, in order to prevent any attempt at poisoning. The whole party had been cautioned against giving any alarm under a threat of being instantly shot down, but, strange enough, although it was only five o'clock, this motley-looking party of fifteen persons did not appear to attract any attention while passing out of the township. This was all the more strange as the bank is only a few yards from the railway station, and is only separated from the other houses in the vicinity by a small vacant allotment. The three bushrangers were armed to the teeth, Kelly having taken the precaution to secure the only two revolvers there were on the premises, besides five boxes of cartridges, containing 125 rounds.

The party were driven straight towards the Faithful Creek Station, the only incident on the road being the temporary breakdown of Kelly's cart in consequence of the horse falling. Faithful Creek Station having been reached, the whole party were placed in the hut along with the other twenty-two persons, making thirty-seven persons altogether in the custody of the bushrangers. Byrne then took Mr. Scott's watch from him, and the preparations for departure having been completed, Ned Kelly informed the whole party that their movements were closely watched, and that if any of them attempted to leave the hut within three hours of the departure of the gang, they would be shot down. It was then half-past eight o'clock, and Mr. Scott endeavoured to get permission to leave at eleven, but Kelly insisted that they should stay till half-past eleven. Ned Kelly then mounted a fine fresh horse, took the money with him, and was immediately followed by the other three bushrangers. The party remained in the hut till about eleven o'clock, when Mr. Scott and others started for Euroa, which was reached about twelve o'clock, when the matter was immediately reported to the police. On the road between the bank and the station Mr. Scott had a long conversation with Kelly, during which the latter said that he had shot Lonigan, and also displayed a splendid gold watch, which Mr. Scott believes to be the one taken from Sergeant Kennedy. He said that all the movements of the troopers, many of whom he had opportunities of seeing when they little knew it, were known to him, and that he had no fear of their taking him.

Before leaving the station, Edward Kelly left a letter with Mrs. Fitzgerald, addressed to the Legislative Council, with instructions for her to post it without fail. This she did, and the document has reached the hands for which it was intended; and although the full contents have not been made public, yet the general tenor of it is known to have been to the following effect:– If the Council grant a free pardon, the outlaws will leave the Colony; but if it is refused, then they intend filling up the measure of their iniquity, and will stop at nothing to carry out their full revenge until they escape altogether or are shot down. The letter is signed "Edward Kelly, a forced outlaw" and is written in red ink, a bottle of which was found on the table at Younghusband's station after Kelly left. Kelly complains of great injustice having been done his mother and other members of his family by the police. He reiterates his desire only to kill members of the police force, and points out that if he is pursued by officers in disguise he cannot help it if civilians are murdered by mistake. With regard to his sister, he brings grave charges against the police, seeks to show that he and his family have been the victims of a system of persecution at their hands. While for the present he states that if he does not receive the "justice" he asks, he will attack anyone with whom he might come in contact, except the friends of the gang, without compunction or discrimination. The document, which altogether is of a fearful nature, winds up with some lines of doggerel. It is written on about twenty-two pages, and Kelly concludes by saying that he had more to write, but that he was unable to do so unless he robbed for more paper.

It is a noticeable fact in connection with this strange event, that the perpetrators of the robbery were not known throughout to make use of a single "bullocky" or colonially-emphasized expression. The female prisoners, too, were treated with every respect; in fact, to use the words of a Euroa man, one of the prisoners, "They" (speaking of the outlaws) "acted like perfect gentlemen", which may possibly have been a slightly exaggerated description of the proceedings.

When the gang left Younghusband's, they directed their course towards Avenel, in the vicinity of which they rested on Wednesday night, at a distance of some twenty-five miles from the scene of their exploit.

A very improbable story was going the rounds in connection with this fact – namely, that one of the black trackers, having got on their trail among the hills near Avenel, pointed up a certain range, and said to the police, who were following him, "White fellow over there, not far; you go, me 'fraid"; and that thereupon the troopers took a line in quite a different direction.

This is on a par with many of the absurdities that have been circulated relating to both parties, and, to say the least, "requires confirmation".

Soon leaving the neighbourhood of Avenel, the outlaws travelled back towards the Puzzle range and Alexandra, and after a series of tacks, long and short, and some great circle sailing, again anchored in their old haven.

CHAPTER XXIV

"Mystery, half veiled and half revealed."
– Scott

"For hosts may in these wilds abound,
Such as are better missed than found."
– Ibid

It was about noontide on one of those warm, exhausting, sweltry days which, in Victoria, marked the close of the January succeeding the date of the murders, when not a breeze stirred the leaves of the forest, and all nature seemed hushed in breathless repose, when the azure vault of heaven could not boast one little cloud to shelter, even for a moment, in its passage, the parched and weary wayfarer from the fierce and nearly perpendicular rays of an almost tropical sun, that a traveller might have been seen slowly climbing, with weary steps, one of the steepest and most tedious spurs of the south-western slope of the Wombat Ranges. And as, at short and frequent intervals, his feet would slip backwards on the treacherously shifting shingle with clothed the ascent, the objurgatory observations, "not loud but deep", which he occasionally vented relative to the soil he was then treading would have led any unprejudiced listener to the conclusion that the pedestrian, in the course of a nomadic – and probably checkered – existence, had made a choice and varied collection of the rarest oaths and most objective curses that could be found under the flags of Great Britain and the United States of America, or, by any possibility, conceived in that juratory magazine and matrix of anathemas – the Anglo-Saxon brain.

There was nothing strikingly peculiar in the general appearance of the stranger – nothing to make him an object of special notice, had he been met on any ordinary highway or in a settled quarter. Yet his dress and belongings had been carefully considered, and judiciously selected with a special object – namely, the non-attraction of observation in his journey through the bush, by the presentation of hues corresponding as much as possible with the tints displayed by the surface and vegetation of that part of the country through which he desired to pass. For although he was in search of a party of men to whom, notwithstanding the dangerous character they bore, he brought credentials that he felt confident would ensure him not only safety, but welcome, yet there were larger parties, in the service of law and order, to be met with, occasionally traversing the neighbourhood, who were occupied in a similar pursuit – at least it was so said – but with different motives, and whose credentials consisted of central-fire ball cartridges. These he did not wish to come in contact with; not that he had any grounds for fearing them on the score of personal safety, but lest the purpose for which he was making the long and hazardous journey might be frustrated, or, at least, ruinously delayed, by their legalized mode of satisfying their curiosity.

There was nothing marked about the physiognomy or figure of the stranger; of medium height and build, somewhat past middle age, with dark brown hair and beard, hazel eyes, and a fair skin, save for the effects of the weather, he offered no point either of attraction or repulsion likely to induce a passer-by to take a second look at him under everyday circumstances.

In his equipment, however, might have been found sundry articles to excite surprise and speculation in the eyes of many. His dress, to commence at the top, consisted of a broad-leafed, tall, soft felt sombrero, of an obtuse greyish-brown; an ordinary flannel singlet, covered by an olive-green Crimean shirt; trousers of a kind known in the slop-shops as "coloured moles", kept in position by leathern waist-belt, and of a neutral shade, which might be described as dirty chocolate; grey military socks, and a pair of strong lace-up boots – all baggage with which he was encumbered had nothing externally to mark it as unusually strange, but its interior would have discovered some articles not strictly in keeping with the ostensible character of the bearer – namely, a man seeking work; and some would have seemed utterly useless. He carried on his shoulder a single coarse brown blanket, rolled up swag fashion, within the folds of which snugly reposed some tobacco, a maiden bottle of "Three star" brandy, and a bottle, which, though three parts filled with "Long John" whiskey, showed evident signs of having been tampered with and tapped since its purchase. The bottles were carefully wrapped in a few of the most recent copies of the Argus and Age newspapers.

From the two ends of this, fastened together with a saddle strap, depended what is known as a "Sydney pot", containing water, and consisting of a quart billy, the close-fitting lid of which formed a pannican. On the opposite side, slung to a strap passing over the other shoulder, hung a well-worn tourist's bag, made of leather, in one compartment of which were a few well-baked, solid scones, and a lump of hard corned beef; while the other contained two small calico bags, with tea and sugar, also a diminutive binocular field-glass, a good-sized note-book, the four of diamonds from a new pack, an ordinary large empty cardboard pill box, a few long hairs from the tail of a horse, and a bright white-metal table spoon. A coloured cotton pocket-handkerchief in his hat, and a strong clasp knife, some twine, a box of matches, a short black clay pipe, and a small compass in his trousers pockets, bring the inventory to a conclusion.

The traveller continued to pursue his journey up the steep, winding, and – save for woody vegetation – barren spur until, after many involuntary deviations, which caused him to retrace his steps for considerable distances, and drew forth appropriate remarks, he reached the highest summit of the principal elevation in those ranges, known as "Wombat Hill".

Here, after looking round for a while, as if in search for some landmark, he unhitched his swag, and throwing himself wearily at the foot and under the shade of a giant gum tree, he proceeded to indulge in a meditative smoke, after first refreshing exhausted nature with a modest quencher of qualified "Long John".

Reclining thus, drowsily comfortable, under the combined and soothing influences of tobacco and whiskey, his thoughts began to shape themselves into muttered soliloquy, the burden of which seemed to be, "I wonder if it's a sell"; after repeating which two or three times, at intervals, he sprung up sharply, exclaiming, while he re-adjusted his traps, "Well, here goes! I'll see it out anyway, hit or miss". His next Act would have appeared highly mysterious, if not idiotic, to a looker-on, for he proceeded to cut sundry small boughs or springs from the green suckers that were growing around, and these he hastily twisted into a sort of wreath or crown, with which he invested his hat; then, taking out the polished spoon, which reflected the rays of the sun from the back of its bowl, like a convex mirror, he fixed it firmly and diagonally across the front of his novel head-dress, thus leaving himself open – should he meet any of the uninitiated – to the suspicion of having recently escaped from the precincts of the Yarra Bend or some other lunatic asylum. He then took out of his pocket compass, placing it on the ground beside the tree under which he had camped, and stood over it, watching the oscillations of the needle, until that unerring guide subsided into a state of absolute repose.

As soon as this point had been reached, he took up the instrument, and, retaining it in his hand, walked away at a comparatively smart rate, towards the east, evidently counting his paces as he went. When he had achieved the limit he desired, some two hundred yards or more, he stopped, and carefully examined his surroundings for a few minutes; then, having apparently satisfied himself, and made up his mind as to the direction he required to take, he plunged down a rocky declivity which led to the ranges on the north-eastern side of the eminence he had occupied.

V. R. MURDER OF POLICE.

£2,500 REWARD

WHEREAS, by a notice published in the *Government Gazette* bearing date the 30th October 1878, a Reward of FIVE HUNDRED POUNDS was offered by the Government for such information as would lead to the capture of each of the four men therein described charged with the murder of certain members of the Police Force, in the King River District: AND WHEREAS it is decided to increase the Reward for the apprehension of one of the said four offenders, named EDWARD KELLY, from FIVE HUNDRED POUNDS to ONE THOUSAND POUNDS: NOTICE IS HEREBY GIVEN that a Reward of ONE THOUSAND POUNDS will be paid by the Government for such information as will lead to the capture of the said EDWARD KELLY and FIVE HUNDRED POUNDS for each of the other three offenders referred to in the said notice of 30th October last.

This notification is in lieu of that of the 30th day of October 1878 above referred to, which is hereby cancelled.

GRAHAM BERRY,
Chief Secretary.

Chief Secretary's Office,
Melbourne, 13th December 1878.

BY AUTHORITY: JOHN FERRES, GOVERNMENT PRINTER, MELBOURNE.

CHAPTER XXV

"For his particular I'll receive him,
But not one stranger."
- Shakespeare

We may here permit ourselves to imagine the wanderer, for some three hours or so, struggling with the average difficulties which beset a man in such a region while endeavouring to discover a point hitherto unvisited by him, while guided only by verbal instructions referring to natural features of the country – features not only difficult of recognition by a stranger, but also not easily discoverable by anyone, owing to the thickly-timbered, and frequently scrubby, character of the locality. Availing ourselves, then, of the "presto" privilege accorded to anecdotical writers, we next present the mysterious stranger to our readers, standing, with a doubtful and puzzled expression of countenance, in the dry bed of a small and shallow water-course which originated at the convergence of two deep, dark, and thickly timbered gullies, the interstices between the trees being filled with close-growing wattle scrub, interlaced in places, with tough and tangled creepers, which formed an almost impenetrable mass.

After moving several times to the right and left of the stream bed, anxiously and earnestly scrutinizing the details surrounding his position, not only with the naked eye, but also through his field-glass, his face suddenly lighted up with an expression of genuine satisfaction and triumph, on catching a glimpse of the summit of an immense moss-covered and dome-shaped rock that lay embowered, and almost concealed, amid the redundant foliage of the trees on the closely-timbered spur which divided, and at the same time, helped to form the two gloomy gullies recently described.

Opening his travelling bag, he quickly extracted from it the four of diamonds card, and taking off his hat and detaching the spoon from it, he replaced the latter with the playing card, which he fixed firmly, the unsullied face of the pasteboard being turned to the front, and he then put on his hat.

This done, he returned the spoon to his haversack, and sitting down on a log, facing the rock, he pulled out the pillbox and horsehair, which he placed on the log. His next step was to select a long and strong horsehair from his bundle, and after fastening a short piece of rush, from one growing beside him, to one end of it by a loop and knot, pass the hair through a pin-hole in the bottom of the pill box, the piece of rush being inside it, and the hair projecting through the hole in its bottom.

This might, at first sight, have appeared to be a preparation for constructing a simple bush telephone, like that used by the Cingalese, and, in good truth, it was intended to answer a somewhat simular purpose, as will be surmised presently; for, taking the box in his left hand, and drawing the hair steadily between the forefinger and thumb of the right, moistened with saliva, the operator succeeded in producing, at intervals of about a minute, exact imitation of the "Caw-aw-a-ww" of a crow, which was distinguishable at a long distance in the silence of the forest, and which would have been good enough to defy competition on the part of the most accomplished mockingbird to be found amid the leafy solitudes of the Australian Alps.

. He had not been more than a quarter of an hour indulging in this apparently harmless bird-like harmony (?) (which added to the appearance of insanity suggested by his head-gear), when two young men, attired in ordinary stockman's style, but displaying two revolvers each at their belts, stepped lightly forward, simultaneously, from the leafy screen at the mouth of the right hand gully, distant about three chains off, and with guns pointed at the corvine minstrel, cried out – "Put up your hands and stand up!" an order promptly and cheerfully obeyed, as though in gratitude for being allowed the privilege of looking straight into the barrels of two loaded smooth-bores at full-cock, with the animating reflection that there was no sufficiently established guarantee against either or both going off while the inspection proceeded.

The younger of these two new arrivals on the scene, who looked quite a youth, with a feminine, beardless face and a mild expression, lowering his muzzle, then walked up to the traveller, and after convincing himself, by a rapid and skilful search, that he was unarmed (unless he chanced to have utilized his swag as a magazine) told him to drop his hands, and then put his question to him, "How is the pound getting on?" to which the reply was, "There hasn't been any more 'gully-raking' lately, and six head have been released". With an abrupt but civil, "All right, come on", the youth led the way to where his mate (who, seeing all was correct, had thrown his gun across his right shoulder) was standing, and introduced the visitor with the brief remark, "This is the cove".

The three men then, forming Indian file, the traveller in the middle, disappeared amid the intricacies of the gully as suddenly and completely as though the mountain gorge had fairly swallowed them up – or down.

The subsequent movements of that trio on that evening, through the bush, being totally inexplicable without the adjunct of an accurate topographical map of the features of the locality, and such not being in existence, we must leave their peregrinations to the fancies of our readers.

Suffice it to say that in about an hour after they vanished they reached their camping place, which was on an eminence, from whence ran four deep, winding gullies, distant about two miles from their starting point, where the tourist, thoroughly exhausted, was made acquainted by his guide with two other men, who, though not quite so young, were decorated, in the prevailing fashion affected by the clique, with that useful, if not chastely ornamental, style of jewellery manufactured largely by Dean and Adams, Webly, Tranter and Colt.

It was remarkable that the eldest of the party, who seemed about twenty-four years of age, and evidently "bossed" the whole concern, was obviously of the same inquiring turn of mind as his younger comrade; for, of the arrival of him whom, at this stage, we may distinguish as the quest, the following dialogue took place:–

Host – "Have you many hawks down your way?" Guest – "Yes, about the stations". Host – "Did you meet any in these ranges?" Guest – "No". Host – "How's that, do you think?" Guest (after a minute or two's anxious thought, the host whiling away the time by playing with a six-shooter) – "I suppose they'd rather tackle a crippled sheep than a lively wombat". Host – "Right you are, my sonny; chuck down your dunnage. Joe's just going to sling the billy in the cave; we never light a fire here".

Acting instantaneously on the welcome permission, or rather invitation, Mr. Blank went to work to unroll his blanket, and bring to view the unexpected liquid treasures that were so cosily ensconced within its voluminous folds.

These were received with low but earnest acclamation, and the purveyor was favoured with a request from headquarters, which amounted to a command, to set the company an example by indulging in a reasonable "snorter" (and no heeltaps) from each bottle, as a preliminary to the flasks making the round of the mob. This he did, nothing loath; and while the cordial balm was being distributed among the captain, the guest, and the crew, including the look-out man, the scene became gradually enveloped in the dusky robe of night, scarcely relieved by the cheese-paring of a moon then in existence.

For imperative reasons, which could in no way interest the reader, we are bound to draw the curtain of judicious silence over the minutes of the further proceedings; but we are not at liberty to state that the guest was treated with the utmost consideration, and the next morning, after a sound and refreshing night's sleep, having been furnished with all the comforts obtainable from a larder so limited in variety, though plenteous in contents, had a final interview with the host, to whose earnest and impressive remarks he might have seen attentively listening, note-book in hand, while ever and anon he made a hurried but careful entry therein, in each case repeating them aloud for confirmation or correction.

The last fact we have had to record relating to this rather mysterious affair, the unravelment of which we leave to the percpicuity of our readers, is that the adventurous being whose hazardous enterprise we have endeavoured partially to chronicle reached his home safe and well, though rather foot-sore, some two days after the date of the last scene described , well satisfied both with the reception he met with, and the results of his trip through the wilds of the Wombat Ranges, with the outskirts of which only he was previously aquainted; and he declares that, while he lives, he will hear a lively recollection of the root of the weather, as well as a grateful rememberance of the warm reception he met among the hills; the latter, he is want to say, he made sure he would meet with, either of one kind or another.

CHAPTER XXVI

'Polonius. – Give him this money, and these notes, Reynaldo.
Renaldo. – I will, my lord.
Polonius. – You shall do marvellously wisely, good Reynaldo.'
- Shakespeare

While people, relying on reports given in the daily prints, were almost tired of saying, "Well, at last the police are in possession of information which must soon place the Kelly Gang in their hands," they were startled almost, if not quite, into admiration – and certainly into astonishment – by the news that those bold and artful outlaws, making their way through the wonderful cordon of Victorian police and eluding those of New South Wales, had come down from their mountain home (like the Highlanders of old), crossed the border into New South Wales, travelled many miles across a plain and open territory, plundered the branch bank of New South Wales at Jerilderie, held possession of the village for two nights and more than one day, and departed in safety with their ill but cleverly and pluckily-gotten gains, retreating back into Victoria, as being the safest harbour of refuge they could find. The account of the robbery, according to the Argus, is to the following effect, and dated from Jerilderie:—

"Exactly, at midnight on Saturday, the 8th of January, Ned Kelly, Dan Kelly, Hart and Byrne surrounded the police barracks here. Hart, in a loud voice, shouted out to Devine, 'Devine, there's a drunken man at Davidson's Hotel, who has committed murder. Get up at once, all of you!' Constable Richards, who was sleeping in a room at the rear of the premises, replied. (Devine and Richards being the names of the two con-stables stationed at Jerilderie.) He got up, and came round to the front door. During the short interval Devine had got out of bed, and opened the front door, when Kelly told him there was a great row at Davidson's. By this time Richards had appeared. Devine approached Kelly, who presented two revolvers at the policemen, telling them to hold up their hands. Immediately the police were pounced upon by the other men, and secured. Devine and Richards were then placed in the lock-up cell, and Mrs. Devine and children were put into the sitting room. Afterwards Mrs. Devine, in her nightdress, with a candle, was made to go through the premises and deliver up all the fire-arms. After this the gang went into the sitting-room, where they kept watch till morning. The next day, Sunday, there was chapel in the courthouse, distant 100 yards from the barracks. It was the duty of Mrs. Devine to get the courthouse ready for Mass. She was allowed to do so, but was accompanied to the courthouse by one of the Kellys, about ten a.m.; Kelly remained in the courthouse while Mrs. Devine prepared the altar and dusted the forms. When this was done, Kelly escorted her back to the barracks, where the door was closed and the blinds all down. Hart and Dan Kelly, dressed out in police uniform, walked to and from the stables during the day without attracting any notice. When everything had been made secure at the barracks, the Kellys dressed out in police uniform, and on Monday, about eleven o'clock, the two Kellys on foot walked down the street in company with Constable Richards. Hart and Byrne followed on horseback. They walked to the Royal Hotel and saw Mr. Cox, the landlord, when Richards introduced Mr. Cox to Kelly, who said he wanted the rooms in the Royal, and that he intended to rob the bank, but would not do anybody any harm. The other bushrangers were then placed by Ned Kelly at the front part of the hotel, and as the people went in for a drink they were seized and placed in a room, where Dan Kelly acted as sentinel.

About ten minutes past twelve on Monday, the 9th, Mr. Living, the teller of the bank, was sitting at his desk, when he heard footsteps approaching him from the direction of the back door. He at first took no notice, thinking it was the manager, Mr. Tarleton. The footsteps continued approaching him, when he turned round on his office-stool, and noticed a man approaching from the back door. He immediately accosted the fellow, who had his revolver already levelled at him, and on asking the intruder who he was and what right he had to enter the bank by the back way, he answered that he was Kelly, and ordered Mr. Living to bail up. The man, who afterwards turned out to be Byrne, ordered him to deliver up what firearms he had. Living replied that he had none. Young Mackie, who was standing in front of the bank, then came in, when Byrne ordered him (Living) to jump over the counter, which he did. He then told him to come with him into Cox's Hotel, and remarked that they had all the police stuck up. They went into the hotel, where they met Ned Kelly, who asked for Mr. Tarleton, when he was told that he was in his room. They went back to the bank, but could not find the manager in his room. Ned Kelly said to Mr. Living, 'You had better go and find him'. Living then searched, and found the manager in his bath.

"Mr. Living was at first a little alarmed at not finding the manager in his room, and at first thought he had got some clue that the bushrangers were in the place, and had cleared out. On finding the manager in his bath, he said to him, 'We are stuck up; the Kellys are here, and the police are also stuck up'. Byrne then brought Hart, and left him in charge of the manager. After Living had got out of the bathroom, Ned Kelly came and took him into the bank, and asked him what money they had in the bank. Living replied there was between £600 and £700, when Kelly said, 'You must have £10,000 in the bank'. Living then handed him the teller's cash, amounting to about £691. Mr. Elliot, the school-master then went into the bank, and as soon as Kelly saw him he ordered him to jump over the counter. Mr. Elliot replied that he could not, but Kelly made him. They then tried to put the money in the bag, but not having one sufficiently large, Ned Kelly went and brought a bag, and they put the money into it. Kelly asked if they had more money, and was answered 'No'.

"Kelly then obtained the teller's revolver, and again requested more money. He then went to the safe and caught hold of the treasure drawer, and requested to know what was in it, and was told by Living that it contained nothing of any value. Kelly insisted on it being opened, and one of the keys was given to him; but he could not open it, owing to the manager having the second key, which was required to open it. Byrne then wanted to break it open with a sledge-hammer, but Kelly brought the manager from the Royal Hotel, and demanded the key, which was given to him, and the drawer was opened, when the sum of £1,450 was taken out by Kelly and placed in the bag. Kelly then took out a large deed-box and asked what it contained, and was told that the contents consisted of a few documents which were of no use. He replied that he would burn the contents, but Mr. Tarleton argued with him, and Kelly took one document and put it into the bag, and then expressed his intention of burning all the books in the office. He, however, left the rest of the papers, and said he would come back and see if there were any deeds for town allotments. The whole of the party then went into the Royal Hotel. Daniel Kelly was in the bar, and Ned Kelly took two of the party to the back of the hotel, where he made a fire and burned three of four of the bank books. In the meantime Mr. Rankin and Mr.Gill, seeing the bank door open, went in, and were immediately followed by Kelly, who ordered them to bail up. Both gentlemen at once made off – Mr. Rankin running into the hotel, and Mr. Gill in some other direction. Ned Kelly ran after Rankin, and caught him in the hotel. Kelly caught him by the collar, and asked him why he ran away, at the same time telling him to go into the passage, and that he intended to shoot him. He took Mr Rankin into the passage, and, after straightening him against the wall, levelled his revolver at him. Several persons called out to Kelly not to fire, and he did not. He then called Hart by the name of Revenge, and told him to shoot the first man that attempted any resistance, and told Rankin that if he attempted to move he would be the first shot. Kelly then asked for Gill, and took Richards and Living with him to look for Gill. The policeman had his revolver with him, but Kelly had previously drawn the cartridges.

"Mr. S. Gill, journalist, when called upon to stand, being frightened ran away, and planted himself in the creek. Ned Kelly, in company with Mr. Living and Constable Richards, came over to the printing office, when Richards said, "Mrs. Gill don't be afraid, this is Kelly". Mrs. Gill replied, "I am not afraid". Kelly said, "Don't be afraid; I won't hurt you nor your husband. He should have not run away". Mrs. Gill replied, "If you shoot me dead, I don't know where Mr.Gill is. You gave him such a fright, I expect he is lying dead somewhere". Mr. Living said, "You see, Kelly, the woman is telling you the truth". Kelly said, "All I want him for is to print this letter, the history of my life, and I wanted to see him to explain it to him". Mr. Living said, "For God's sake, Kelly, give me the papers and I will give them to Gill". Mr. Living under promise then received the papers. This is given as I received it from Mrs. Gill, who, though alarmed, never evinced any fear.

"The party next went to McDoughall's Hotel, where Kelly took a blood mare out of the stable, and remarked that he would return it in three weeks. The party then went to the telegraph office, and met Byrne, who had cut the wires. Ned Kelly then broke the insulators at the office with his revolver. After this, he took the postmaster and his assistant to the Royal Hotel, and left the party there. Kelly returned to the bank, and obtained a saddle and a pair of riding trousers belonging to Mr. Tarleton, and also a watch and a gold chain. The saddle was put on the mare, and Dan Kelly mounted it and rode away, but returned in five minutes. Dan Kelly and Hart then both kept guard at the hotel. Ned Kelly informed the postmaster Mr. Jefferson, that if he attempted to mend the wires before next day, or offered any assistance, he would be shot. He also told Mr. Jefferson that he intended to take him a few miles in the bush, and then liberate him. He informed those present that he intended sticking up the Urana coach that night, and would shoot anyone who attempted to give warning. He rode off in the direction of the Murray, with the money, and in the meantime Mr. Tarleton had succeeded in despatching a messenger to Urana to warn the bank manager there. The remaining part of the gang then rode in the direction of the police camp, and the party were liberated and Mr. Living started for Deniliquin.

"The following additional particulars are given by Mr. Tarleton, the manager of the bank. That gentleman states that at the time of the occurrence he had not long returned from long ride of 40 miles, and was having a bath, when the teller came rushing into the bathroom and exclaimed that they were stuck up. Mr. Tarleton at first thought it rubbish, but, on seeing two men with revolvers, believed such to be the case. As soon as he came out of the bath, Hart pointed a pistol at him and then searched his clothes. Mr. Tarleton made some inquiries as to the movements of the gang, but Hart, after answering one or two questions replied in an angry voice that Mr. Tarleton had better cease asking questions. Hart then took him into the hotel, and as he was going in he noticed Byrne strike the Chinese cook. He was then placed with some others in a bar parlour, where he was kept until taken back to the bar. Hart stood the whole time at the door of the room with revolvers, and evinced a strong desire to shoot somebody occasionally if there was a little too much talking in the room. During his confinement in the room, Mr. Tarleton was placed in such a position that he thinks he could have knocked Hart down, but on asking the policeman if he would back him up, he replied that Dan Kelly had them covered with his revolver, and if he happened to miss them he would be sure to kill some of the others.

"The gang then prepared to go, but before doing so, Ned Kelly made a speech, with the evident intention of exciting pity. He said that on the occasion when Fitzpatrick, the Benalla constable, was shot, he was not within 400 miles of Greta, and during his carrier he had stolen 280 horses from Whitty's station, and sold them; and beyond this he had not been guilty of any other crime. The horses, he stated, were sold to Baumgarten. Kelly showed those present his revolvers, and pointed out one which he said was the property of Constable Lonigan, and further stated that the musket which he shot Lonigan with was an old worn-out crooked thing. He asked those present if they would like to be treated as he had been treated, and detectives to go to their houses and present revolvers at their mothers and sisters and threaten to shoot them if they did not say where Ned Kelly was. He considered such treatment to be more than any man could stand, and was enough to make him turn an outlaw. He said that he came to that place, not with the intention of robbing the bank, but to shoot the two policemen, Devine and Richards, who were worse than any black trackers, especially Richards, whom he intended to shoot immediately. Mr. Tarkleton remarked to Kelly that it was Richard's duty, and he should not blame him for doing it. Kelly then replied, 'Suppose you had your revolver ready when I came in, would you not have shot me?' Mr. Tarleton replied, 'Yes'. 'Well', said Kelly, 'that's just what I'm going to do with Richards —shoot him before he shoots me'. The party then interceded for Richards, but Kelly said – 'He must die!' Kelly then started to walk in the direction of the police camp, in company with Richards. Hart and Dan Kelly rode up the street, shouting and flourishing their revolvers. The captives were then free. Both the Kellys were dressed as troopers. Before leaving, Ned Kelly remarked that he had made a great blunder in connection with the affair, which would likely be the means of capturing the gang. Byrne was put in possession of the plunder obtained from the bank, and he left Jerilderie an hour before the others, proceeding in the direction of Tocumwal – that is, he took the direct road back to Victoria".

During the Monday, Hart asked where Curtain, the auctioneer, was, as they came, he said, on purpose to shoot him, and would have shot Richards and Devine, but that Mrs. Devine begged them off.

Fortunately the auctioneer had started for Urana at an early hour in the morning.

About two in the afternoon, Byrne galloped over to the telegraph-office and found Mr. Jefferson, the post and telegraph master, standing on the verandah. He said he was Kelly, and ordered Jefferson inside, presenting his revolver at the same time. He then cut the wires, and remained in the office till Ned Kelly came over from the Royal Hotel, threatening to shoot Jefferson if he offered to touch the instrument. Kelly got eight of the telegraph poles cut down, smashing the insulators himself with his revolver, and warning the postmaster that he would be shot if he attempted to send a message before Wednesday. After Byrne had got well away with the money, Kelly shouted for 30 or 40 people at McDougall's Hotel. The Rev. Mr. Gribble having complained to Kelly that Hart had taken a silver watch from him, that promising young gentleman was obliged to return it (under a threat of shooting) by his captain, who advised his subordinate to get a good watch when he was about it, if he wanted one – at the same time addressing him as "a thing". Mr. Doughall's mare was returned to him on a remonstrance being offered to Ned Kelly who, when he rode off from McDoughall's Hotel, after shouting for all hands and the cook, called out "Hurrah for the good all times of Morgan and Ben Hall!" He was loudly cheered on his departure by the crowd, with whom he seemed to be a great favourite, doubtless for his pluck, liberality, and jollity of manner.

The Victorian and Sydney police authorities were said to be exerting all they energies towards the capture of this ubiquitous gang, and there is no doubt that the reward of £2,000 per head now placed on them by the two Governments jointly, must increase the chance of their being betrayed by treachery into the hands of justice; but until they either are arrested (or make good their escape altogether), we, for our part, will not place much reliance on the now, as it were, stereotyped reports of their being surrounded, tracked, or what not, by the police "or any udder man".

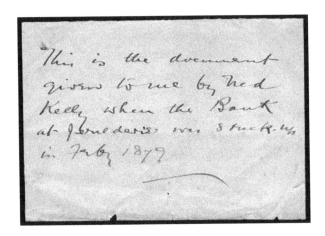

CHAPTER XXVII

"Honest, my lord?"
- Othello

To all right-minded and law-abiding men it must seem in the highest degree desirable, both from a moral and social point of view – in accordance with justice and policy – that evil-doers should meet their deserts in proportion to the enormity of their several offences, not only with a view to punishing the culprits, but also with the object of discouraging others from inflicting injuries upon society similar to those for which the offenders are made to suffer; and it is satisfactory to reflect that, under our advanced state of Jurisprudence, a miscarriage of justice is the rare exception and not the prevailing rule.

Yet we could wish to notice that as much energy was exhibited in capturing and prosecuting those criminals for whose apprehension no reward is offered as those whose arrest or conviction is the harbinger of a golden return.

To the observing, conscientious, impartial and reflective mind, too it must prove a source of regret that a vast amount of wickedness is committed within the bounds of the law, not only with impunity, in many cases, but so long as the result be a successful one, with credit and honour to the perpetrator in others. For instance, how many beings have to be done to death by a continued course of systematic cruelty, spread over a sufficient space of time to elude the charge of murder or manslaughter! How many men - aye, and women – have been killed, and quickly, by the impure and poisonous drinks retailed in some "shanties" and public houses by unscrupulous proprietors, whose purveyors must be as themselves! In how many systems have the seeds of disease and death been sown by the manufacturers and vendors of mischievously adulterated articles or food! What cures may have been frustrated, and deaths caused, by the sale and administration of inferior and adulterated drugs! What fatal results must sometimes be brought about by the use of many of the quack nostrums we see daily advertised!

How many men, again, have risen to opulence and eminence in commerce circles by their acquaintance with and unscrupulous use or what are termed by an unmerited euphemism, "tricks of trade", a term which is in reality a synonym for "cowardly robbery of the public!" It is, however, for obvious reasons, only the man whose "word is his bond" in buying, that can with impunity continue to retain his character while carrying on this system of spoliation in selling, and this fortunately forms a wholesome check on the number of such plunderers. It is to be hoped that such practices are, through competition, on the wane, and we believe such is the case, or we might endorse the poet's dictum –

"And honour fades where commerce long holds away".

The worthy, truly admirable, and really pious Bishop of Melbourne, whose principles and teachings are evidently based upon those of the Founder of his religion, rather than in accord with the generality of that Founder's professing followers, is reported to have made the following remark in connection with the perpetrators of the murders in the Wombat Ranges, when addressing a meeting at Mansfield:– "We should pity the poor wretches who have caused us to mourn over the recent disasters". We fancy that even he might have felt disposed to add the word "despise", had he been referring to such miscreants as we have first spoken of as sinning within the law, though sometimes shaving the boundary.

It is strange that while every one subscribes to the proverb, "Honesty is the best policy", so many bow the knee to successful roguery. Surely it must be that dishonesty is not dishonest while it commands prosperity, as –

"Treason never prospers, this the reason –
That when it prospers 'tis no longer treason".

THE END

CPSIA information can be obtained
at www.ICGtesting.com
Printed in the USA
LVHW102201120522
718633LV00008B/369